LEARNING TO
SURVIVE
LIVING IN TWO WORLDS

Zacharia Korn

To order additional copies of this book, contact:
Xlibris
1-888-795-4274
www.Xlibris.com
Orders@Xlibris.com

Contents

PREFACE v

PROLOGUE viii

DEDICATION xiii

1-BACKGROUND 1

2-THE BRIDE TALES 11

3-THE GROOM`S STORIES 21

4-BUNKER & PARTISANS 29

5- IN THE ARMY 35

6-ARE YOU A COMMUNIST? 39

7-SWITCHING SIDES 49

8-THE CAMP 57

9 – THE NANNY 65

10-DESTINATION UNKNOWN 79

11-CHANGE OF PLANS 87

12- IN ITALY 95

13 - ACT OF FAITH 107

14-BON VOYAGE 113

15-BACK TO THE SEA 127

16 -ARICA, SAND AND SEA 133

17- NANNY RITA 141

18 – THE CHOLITAS 145

19-BIBLIOGRAPY 150

20 - GLOSSARY 151

PREFACE

This story was written based on facts, conversations with WW2 refugees, including neighbors in the Foerhenwald Displaced Persons Camp, reports, reading books, researching historical data from Wikipedia, memories of what I was told, or believe so, or sort of remember; magazines, articles that I have read and others.

From Polish public school till the election of Pope John Paul II (Karol Wojtyla) my mother (ZL) had good memories; I presume so; because our conversations were a bit of a mixture of bad memories and good ones) and she liked these Polish memories in general; although not all of them.

She sometimes talked about it for a specific reason; to make a comparison between events now and then, to comment news or to justify something.

The good memories were a tiny part of her wartime memories. Most of them were not pleasant memories and an issue that repeatedly popped up was the way Polish Jews were treated by some of the Polish gentile community, especially those considered her neighbors, in her own town.

Although many Polish people helped and risked their lives for helping Jews and other minorities in World War II, she felt that most people she knew failed as humans. Some events she witnessed and some she was told by people she trusted and believed.

From my father's (ZL) side his memories seemed neutral.

In the sense that they were just memories, and he didn't make his feelings too public. He did not care much about being Polish born when talking about Poland or his youth; probably because he disliked his memories.

Basically, opposite feelings to those of my mother that made a point of knowing and saying she liked the Polish National Anthem as a proof of her apparent openness and school time patriotism.

Memories from my father's side were maybe more complete; I spent nearly two months travelling around the world with him and having a chat about war years at least once a day. These chats were in an aeroplane, in a hotel or a restaurant.

This book pretends to tell a story of common Jewish people whose origins were from Poland's Tarnogrod families thru the eyes of my parents.

Families that survived the ugly part of history that was the Holocaust, and who managed to recreate for themselves a second life, after having kept their first life dormant and its long term memories widely distributed throughout their brain's cortex.

The Nazi idea of wiping out a whole community of people that have in common a written tradition and a set of moral and ethical rules was bizarre and stinks rotten, but remains.

From my personal experience, very little to be honest, except the fact to have been born in Camp Foehrenwald, Town of Wolfratshausen, Bavaria, Germany. Therefore did not contribute much.

After the Second World War (WW2),when the above mentioned slave labor Camp became a Displaced Persons Camp, we lived there until I was two years old; period of which I don't have a living memory, I think they call it "child's amnesia"; only memories of events told by my parents later and some photos.

My parents spent over five years at this Camp; although both were from Tarnogrod they met at this Camp in Bavaria, married and had a son.

I tried to keep close to the stories and comments that my parents made, either when a story was told or when questions were answered.

Maybe it would have been more truthful if I ever kept notes or tapes; but I did not and it is my memory that I must trust now.

All names are just invented and do not have any relation with already passed away or living persons; but by coincidence they seemed to be close to reality. Nobody that talked to me suspected that their information would turn to be part of a book. Neither did I suspect to write, on this topic, a book one day.

To make it easier and avoid repetition the following names are used:

-Majer: Father.

-Roza: Mother.

-Sjandla: Grandma

I apologize if its contents hurt feelings or bring bad memories, also if some events seem untrue, made up or exaggerated.

Whatever the reason, the intention was to tell the story in a didactic manner that could be considered historical fiction or fiction with a story to tell. It doesn't need to be a mirror image of reality but it is fiction-real in our minds and in the minds of those who survived WW2.

To be fair, some stories and comments about the Displaced Persons Camp were heard from some people very close to my family, already in heaven, that when talking to me during a lunch, dinner or having a coffee would remember something from the past, being treated in this book, and just said or commented it.

Some information came from people that were our neighbors in Foehrenwald Camp southwest of Munich; that I spent a lot of my time with them while I was a teenager.

Not for the book`s sake or anything in special.

Just pure conversation, many stories I must have forgotten, but the process of writing has brought them out again or it had triggered an invention process based on what I heard or read. This process worked like placing pavement on a road full of holes.

My parents and their generation learnt to survive and later realized they had lived in two different worlds, before and after WW2.

My generation has dealt with elegant anti-Judaism where they tell you that you don´t look Jewish, you are a different type of Jew, did not know there are black Jews and so on.

The purpose of this book is to try to keep memories alive.

Never forget!

São Paulo, February, 01, 2019.

PROLOGUE

Since their birth, in Tarnogrod, Poland, destiny played the biggest role in writing a story of young people from reasonably average Jewish origins, born in a small town inhabited mostly by Jewish craftsmen and Gentile farmers.

At a quick glimpse thru history, to serve as a background we had:

In the Middle Age's period of western history, Polish rulers invited Jews to come and live with them because most Jews were craftsmen and this was an activity that nobility understood to be essential to any country at that time. Locals, non Jewish, were mainly farmers.

Centuries later, the same welcoming land concentrated the ghettos of Warsaw, Lodz and others; and continued with the extermination Camps of Auschwitz, Treblinka, Belzec, Sobibor and others. True, the Camps were idealized and operated mainly by the Germans.

The Holocaust happened because conditions for it to occur were ripe, and these conditions were some of the strongest collective brain washing accumulated actions of all times. One important condition was the support given by western governments to the Nazi and fascist type regimes against the communist threat coming from the soviets and potentially from within the various European countries. This attitude allowed the Nazi regime to go ahead with their ideology, the intention to build a fascist empire and degenerate actions.

Racist ideology came in as a wave and for Jews it became a loose or loose proposition. If the person was against bankers, he considered most bankers to be Jewish therefore he was against Jews. It also followed that all rich were Jews; to others, intellectuals, artists, poets and writers were communists and also Jews were poets, artists, thinkers and these were all communists. Then Jews were communists.

In times of misery and hardship, wrong choices make the fuel needed for a fire. Anything can be the spark. Coming from a military disaster and emerging badly wounded as a result of WW1 they selected the guilty parties: the Jewish people. In their practicing ideology, first they needed to eliminate the Jews and next conquer the world.

A similar thought to that belief of the coming of the Messiah and the end of civilization as we know it.

Going back in time, persecutions of Jews started basically in large scale with the Crusades (XI century till XIII). After accumulating centuries of lies, hatred and some preachers that specialized in keeping people united thru hate for Jews and Muslims, helping second class nobility, those 'without inheritance' because the tradition was mostly everything for the first born, to conquer new lands and new kingdoms.

The crusaders on their way to Jerusalem, robbed, murdered, tortured and maimed Jewish people and other minorities. All these 'hate activities' done under the organized help of preachers that were always present to guarantee that everything done was "in the name of the Lord". Preachers, with behavior problems and psychotic ideas, but very popular with ignorant crowds and useful for the elites.

The Crusades were, at the beginning of the second millennium, a spark strong enough to create a culture of intolerance and a system of belief that together with political power tried to dominate the world.

Gone was the Roman Empire and in its place grows the Holy Roman Empire. Finally, a Christian Empire, in the place of the Roman Empire.

Politically useful for the holders of power, since striving to have unified countries or kingdoms, they used any means and an important one was hate for foreigners, nowadays called xenophobia; especially those with strong culture and traditional systems. These were harder to incorporate.

Don't get it wrong: long before the Crusades the ideology of unity in a kingdom or a country was already creating a system where the "we" were to be united and "they" may join us under certain restrictions.

Four hundred years later "The Holy Inquisition" was the natural grandchild of the crusades.

In the XV – XVI centuries, the Spanish Inquisition tortured, converted to Catholicism and killed non-Christian minorities, but brutality still opened a small window for "convert and you will be one of us". For survival many did convert. Considering we are dealing with human beings the few options given transformed in all kinds of combinations.

Soon after, not even conversion was sufficient.

A destroying machine made of thousands of people was placed in operation to solve the 'Jewish Question'. In the year 1666 a Cossack uprising massacred over one hundred and fifty thousand Jews living in Ukraine.

The strange combination was also there: social unrest due to rich Polish landlords land rentals, Jesuits against Orthodox Christians in a religious dispute and Jewish people in the middle, working, learning, studying and trying to survive.

Selected as a permanent target, the final conclusion, for the racist anti-Jews herd was the complete destruction of the Jewish people.

That is why we need to participate in the effort of "NEVER FORGET" so it doesn't have a chance to happen again. This paranoiac idea of destroying the Jews apparently came from the first Crusade and its popular leaders, the crazy preachers (early second Millennium). Historically it started in large scale in the IV century or from earlier times.

Its created beast, racism, periodically showed up to the public. A few chose to accept it and so was in the past, a few.

But many joined forces when their highly educated brains short circuited into making them killers. Blood thirsty killers, and plain bureaucratic killers. The last ones cold blooded order followers that never discussed reasons; just complied.

The Holocaust was the adopted child of the Inquisition that thru hundreds of years was being practiced

ix

thru the 'Progroms'. I believe a Yiddish word of Russian language origins, that means a 'violent riot' aimed at persecution and massacre of Jews and ethnic minorities.

When there were no Jews available in a certain place, antisemitism was available there. To hate you didn't need the object of your hatred near you. The idea was enough. The process was that of a believer: having faith; in this case, an ill faith.

A great part pointing to the Jews was historically played by the early Catholic Church and their supported monarchies and royal houses, such as the Bourbons, the Habsburgs and others.

These "houses", for a question of power, having considered themselves to reign in the name of God, normally segregated Jews, Muslims, Gypsies and other minorities. The House of Bourbon, House of Habsburgs and specially Tsar Alexander of Russia had big influence in having reversed the equality laws imposed by Napoleon in all countries eventually controlled by the French after their revolution and empire build up.

Once Napoleon was exiled in Elba, the monarchists started moving to cancel the minority protection laws.

After Waterloo's defeat followed by the exile of the emperor in St. Helena Island, definitively went backwards by having either cancelled or ignored the emancipation laws.

Many sick human brains can be transformed into a pack of blood thirsty wolves. To breed a blood thirsty animal, that kills to satisfy himself, is against human nature.

The question is: who were the people that brought these bloody wolves and why? Unfortunately there is no easy or immediate answer but one of them could be your neighbor.

I suspect that a sophisticated form of jealousy plays an important role. How come such a small group of people become the chosen people and play such a key role in monotheist religion?

Why did God give this tiny group the ten commandments, the Bible, Moses, the prophets, Jesus and the Apostles? Because they elected themselves, to be the chosen people. For sure, at the time, nobody else wanted.

Chosen to suffer, to be enslaved, to receive God's selected land and finally chosen to do the best for mankind and repair and improve the world.

But we need to survive, that is the biological reason we live for.

'NEVER FORGET' will help avoid repetition of the horrors of the Holocaust.

Educate for tolerance at home and at school. We must give our contribution by being always intolerant to racism even in our spare time.

We need to start at home.

Finally I need to request public sympathy for a candidacy to the Peace Nobel Price for ZEGOTA – Children Section, who rescued over two thousand five hundred Jewish children in the city of Warsaw;

mostly rescued out from the Ghetto. It´s a totally independent appeal since I do not belong formally to ay fan club or similar

I hope you enjoy reading this book and when finished, it has made you interested in the subject; then it is a winner.

Before the reader starts speculating if this book is fiction let me announce: this book can be classified as historical fiction.

The sense in which this happened was a mixture of real academic history,

Newspapers´ articles, various books, personal; to feel-in gaps (in knowledge or memory), so end result: historical fiction.

Thanks for reading me, I hope you enjoy it.

Writing on this book finished on December, 2018 and revision on Jan/15th/2019.

All the best

Zacharia Korn São Paulo, February, 1st, 2019.

"I will speak a little about the Identity Pathology, in the social sense of the word. What is identity in this sense?

It is a word that comes from the Latin 'Idem', which means 'the same thing', that means (in the social sense), identity. It is that what we have in common with other persons with whom we form a group.

The search for identity is innate to human beings. The human being is a gregarious being. He tries to get closer to other human beings, and searches for identification signals with them, something that will make them be closer to that group. That is the process of an Identity being born."

(Moacyr Scliar – Brazilian writer and Medical Doctor – From de article Jewish Identity – Dilemmas and Possibilities from the book History´s Tribunal –Judging the controversies of Jewish history - Relume Dumara – Jewish History and Culture Centre -2005.- Free translation by myself)

DEDICATION

This book is especially dedicated to my parents, Majer Korn (ZL) & Roza Haller de Korn (ZL).

Most of it was idealized based on them. I guess they would have disagreed in making public these stories and themselves as main characters but they would have confirmed every word of its contents.

Nevertheless, I am sure they would have enjoyed the fact that I wrote this book.

Thru these stories I pay tribute to those human beings who suffered from intolerance from other fellow humans.

Dedicated to my wife Sandra and son Rafael

1-BACKGROUND

Poland and the history of Jews in Poland.

The Polish nation began to be built in the 10th century A.C., on lands in Central Europe ruled by a people called Piasts. Their leader, Mieszko, converted into Christianity in 966 A.C. and was followed by most of his people.

The first massive migration of Jews into Poland happened in 1098, coincidently the year of the first crusade. The total period considered was from 1095 till 1099 A.C. In Europe the worst attacks to Jewish communities occurred in Medieval Germany.

In 1102 A.C. the Polish King decided to divide the country into two, for his sons; measure that weakened the new country and created facilities for others to divide and conquer.

In the XII and XIII centuries, the rulers of central Europe had a policy of building more towns and enlarging existing ones by bringing neighboring German people to live in and bring their manual and scientific abilities.

The second Crusade period was from 1146 till 1149.

Third and fourth Crusades occurred between 1189 till 1192 and, 1199 till 1204.

The Crusades were a great impact on Jewish life in Europe, wherever the large numbers of followers passed and also on the Middle East where not only Jews were persecuted but also Muslims, in such a deep rooted manner that it is still remembered and taught in the Arab world. From an intellectual point of view it is pointed out as a long lasting anti-Muslim motivation catalyst.

Expropriation, compulsory religious conversion and robbery were routine; but let´s clarify, the hatred was directed by the crusaders to the Christians and other religions.

As a coincidence at the same period of time a Jewish mystical movement began in central Europe in what is Germany in modern days.

This movement is called 'Khassidei Ashkenaz' that means 'the Hassidim of Ashkenaz' or 'The German Pietists', and was originated by religious pious people from two Jewish families:

The Kalonymos family, that had roots in the north of Italy and the Abun, originally from Provence, southern France. These families migrated to what is now Germany in the X th century.

The movement was at its highest point in the XII and XIII centuries.

Being a product of this mystical movement, Rabbi Juda Ha-Hasid, who lived and guided his followers from Regensburg was their spiritual leader. They were a Jewish mystical, ascetic movement.

Going a step further in history, in 1241, Poland was invaded by the Mongols who finally did not enjoy the country and withdrew shortly, in 1242.

Next invaders were the Teutonic Knights that started to conquer various pagan lands in Central Europe and in 1308 Ac initiated a long lasting series of wars that lasted about two hundred years. As an example we have the following Polish - Teutonic Wars:

1308-1309 – Teutonic takeover of Danzig

1326-1332 – Concluded by the Treaty of Kalisz in 1343

1409-1411 – Polish-Lithuanian-Teutonic War ; in 1414; - Hunger War

1422 – Gollub War ; 1431-1435 – Lithuanian Civil War;

1454 – 1466 – Thirteen Year's War; 1467 – 1479 - War of the Priests

1519 – 1521 – Retterkrieg.

This Germanic chivalry Order, the Teutonic Knights was a military-religious order that originally took care of German soldiers of the Crusades in and out of the Holy Land.

Similar to the order of the Templars and the Chevaliers Hospitaliers, all members were from noble families and had monastic bows. Apparently lived a very simple life of a warrior dedicated to God, no luxury, no palaces, but the order accumulated wealth in land in gold and silver and at some stage in European history their leaders competed with established Kings and even Popes.

Going back in history so that we have a larger background:

In the XIVth century under Kazimierz the Great (1333-1370) the Polish Lords obtained total control of the land and expanded into Russia. Kazimiercz was a reformer, founded the first university and became known as a protector of Jews whose community enlarged rapidly.

He invited Jews to live and work in Poland during many years (1333-1350).

In the next two centuries the Polish nobility increased their individual power while the various Kings were weakened by the smart policies pushed by the Polish nobility.

Many invasions followed: Teutonic Knights as mentioned before (in 1410 and in 1453) and unrest and lack of unity occurred for many years in various arenas; religion, politics, royalty, taxes and laws about land ownership. Until Invaded peacefully by the Order of the Jesuits, in 1560.

These highly qualified preachers made a big effort in unification thru Christianity and the permanent teaching of it.

In 1568, the city of Krakow, lost the right to be the capital city of Poland, honor given to Warsaw.

In 1569, King Sigismund II Augustus issued an edict called 'De Non Tolerandis Judaeis' whereby Jews were forbidden to sell, buy, build houses, own land and others. It was abolished by King Stephen Bachory in 1580.

In 1572, when the last Jagienollian king died, monarchy became elective. The elective assembly that voted was composed of nobles only.

Henry Valois, a Frenchman, was elected King of Poland in May 1573.

Strange but reasonably common when noble families have no interest; either because the chance of making riches is low or because noble thieves had already stolen most of the land's treasury.

His brother Charles IX, was King of France, and died in 1574. Henry Valois, the king, retired from Poland and went back to France to become King of France again.

The nobility of Poland elected Anna and her groom to be, Stefan Batoly, Queen and King in 1575 and they remained like that until 1586.

In the 16th century occurred many religious-political events based on protestant Reform and Catholic Counter-Reform.

New invasions occurred in the 17th century by Sweden and in the 18th century by Russia. The neighboring countries started taking parts of the country (Russia, Prussia and Austria) and economic decline continued.

When Napoleon I passed in 1807 on his way to invade Russia, many Polish nationals joined the French armies and fought against the Russians.

Napoleon supported Polish popular wish to become and independent nation. This lasted until Napoleon's death in 1821 in the island of St. Helena.

Poland was divided again and dominated most of the time by the Russians.

The Ghettos, where most Jews lived, studied, worked and prayed were liberated by Napoleon Bonaparte's troops and Jews obtained the rights, before denied to them, basically freedom to live outside the Ghetto and participate openly in commercial activities.

The Napoleon Wars (1804-1815) emancipated the Jews of Western Europe. When the Napoleonic wars started, the Jewish people that lived in Europe were politically and economically marginalized and physically contained in the Ghettos.

With the emancipation laws, Jews were allowed, for the first time, to enter European society, prosper and cause a major impact in their societies thru their integration and also thru secularization, assimilation and conversion into Catholicism.

A few steps backwards were given by Napoleon under pressure by some advisors, pressure from significant part of the clergy and nobility; some important allies, issued in 1808, a restrictive decree limiting freedom of Jews that lasted for a few months and was formally removed in 1811 under the condition that nothing distinguished a Jew from a non-Jew.

Most of this reverting trend was supported, thru international diplomatic pressure, by Tsar Alexander who was a fiercely anti-Jewish, had large following within nobility and promoted religious and civil persecutions and by some members of the nobles Habsburg House.

In the Napoleonic years, Jewish children were permitted to attend general schools, Jewish men were accepted in the army, and Jews were granted citizen status.

Rebellions occurred again in 1830 and 1863. Severe discrimination and antisemitism were growing. Emigration to Russia and to the United States began around 1880.

The fact that called for attention, is that Hasidic leaders tried strongly to persuade Jews to remain in Eastern Europe. They thought the worst would come from Western Europe and the United States. These societies were considered too open and secular; Hasidism was conservative but also surprising; it carried a message of love, it meant 'loving kindnesses. You love God and are loved by him'.

We could say it was a hint for the future "flower power" of the hippies.

But coming from such a conservative group it seemed a miracle.

Freedom came again for a short time after World War I (1914-1918). Some token attitudes with regards to Jewish people occurred after WW1 when political representatives of the new state, called Poland, signed minority clauses giving the Jewish people in Poland equal rights. It turned out to be worthless.

When the German troops, came marching in 1939, there were over three and a half millions Jews in Poland and the largest concentration of Hasidic Jews in the world. What made a historical and cultural difference was that in WW! Jews fought for their "King and Country" and not for religious causes. But if it is good it normally doesn't last long.

World War I heated the antisemitism wave in Europe; especially with the Germans. Being the big losers of the Great War and still they considered to be better than the rest of Europe, the Germans started searching for reasons, and in the right wing extreme of politics and top of the army the losses were caused by Jews and Communists.

After the war the main reasons cultivated by the Anti-Semitic right wing were the Jews, Communists (normally mixed with Jews) and the Versailles treaty System (Not necessarily Jewish).

This was already being prepared during the War, in 1916, when the generals of the German military prepared a report called "Judenzahlung" (Jewish Census) that basically was set to prove that: Jews did not fight, did not risk their life for the motherland.

It would measure how many Jews of military age were in the front and how many in the rear, during World War I.

The results were that about eighty percent of male Jews in military age were in the front. The military promptly decided to keep the report secret! In the 1920's and 1930's the overall poor economy caused Jewish people to live in poverty as it did with the non-Jewish population.

The elitist thinking in Germany was well-known and followed by the polish right wing elements of society. In the Polish church there was a widespread anti-Jewish feeling inherited from the times of the Teutonic Knights invasion and the Jesuits pacific invasion.

Jews were regarded, as in other countries, as foreigners. It was not considered if their ancestors had been in the land for many years before.

It was a democratic view: all Jews were the same, regardless of age, sex, educational level. Polish nobility used to exploit their land with peasant labor very near to being under a slaver system, was overspending, underpaying and forcing their manpower to be silently obedient.

In God's name the members of nobility forced an obedience system; it was there available but unused with time.

The routine churchgoing by their peasants and listening to incendiary speeches by blood thirsty preachers on how the Jews were guilty of Deicide and bringing down on everybody dark days of suffering and the solution was prayer and a deep belief in their religious leaders who also had their masters in nobility.

This was the controlling structure: Nobility was related to the Catholic church´s higher levels and later to the rich families too. The church´s structure guided the crowds and education was in the hands of their members who taught the rich and noble.

This way, perpetuated the intolerance and certain virtual truths that were repeated at home and passed on to the people in general.

Slowly, anti-Jewish attitudes emerged and measures in an Anti-Semitic environment were done through revoked citizenship, limited access to universities and professions. In this environment, Hitler´s army invaded Poland on September, 1ˢᵗ, 1939, and started World War II.

This was probably one of the darkest times in Europe when the Nazi party publicly showed the world what they meant and how badly they wanted to eliminate the Jewish Question. Most of the world sat on their back and while the SS and the SA disputed the title of "Kings of Brutality" by breaking windows, painting walls, harassing old women and men.

Soon after the German invasion, the Polish army was crushed. The German military first entered the town of Likew, next door to Tarnogrod, and it was the second day of Rosh Hashana, the Jewish New Year, on a Friday afternoon.

In less than a month the Polish government fled into exile and the army surrendered to Germany on September, 27ᵗʰ.

At the same time Poland became Hitler´s partner, since they had signed a non-aggression pact, The Soviet Union, also invaded part of Poland. Between the two of them they partitioned Poland in three areas.

One for each and a third area sort of independent but really under the claws of both the Soviets and the Germans.

The German army showed their teeth rapidly: tens of thousands of polish intellectuals were killed.

Germans regarded Poles as "sub-human" and Polish Jews somewhere lower than this.

The program planned by the Germans for the Polish Jews (and any other Jews that could be found) was one of concentration first, isolation next and finally annihilation.

Concentrated and isolated in Ghettos, walled cities within Polish cities where conditions were so bad that illness and infectious diseases weakened and killed people every day.

When they were already debilitated the remaining Jews were deported to concentration Camps built to exterminate people in an industrial scale.

Some of the anti-Jewish measures that the Germans took in Poland were:

-Jews were liable for forced labor. Simple slavery (Oct/1939): Opened the selection process of people for slave work and for concentration Camps.

-Jews were forbidden in certain city areas and Synagogues were destroyed; anticipated the advance of the Ghettos, limiting where Jews can be or go.

-In November, 1939: Must identify every Jew with a star in a yellow arm band, and so continued the selection process; you could see a Jew from any distance.

-Created a Jewish Council; control over Jews (Facilitates the process of extermination). Jews being selected by other Jews.

-Jewish bank deposits frozen: Clearly stole monies being prepared and made it difficult for Jews to run away.

-Jews cannot change residence (Dec/1939).Continued movement in the direction of limited access and corralled Jews.

-Curfew for Jews: 9 PM till 5AM. Concentrate Jews and continue to break their will.

-In January/1945-Jews cannot travel by train-Only with special permission.

-1940 saw the first Ghetto built: Lodz, then Warsaw and mass deportation. After concentrating Jews in Ghettos, selection of slave labor, remaining Jews too old, too young and handicapped.

-In 1941: Jews forbidden to leave Ghettos. Already rounded up like cattle, separated and easy to select (slave manpower, experimentation, elimination).

-Gentiles who helped Jews subjected to death penalty: pressure on non- Jews, to avoid escape chances for Jews.

-Death Camps begin operations: Lublin, Kulmhof, Treblinka, Sobibor, Belzec and Auschwitz: Started the German 'final solution' by transporting the remaining Jews to industrial extermination Camps.

-During 1942: Jews from Lublin Ghetto deported to Belzec, three hundred thousand Jews from Warsaw Ghetto deported to Treblinka.

The cycle would repeat itself in shorter periods. Those working in a regime of near starvation had a limited span of life. Once unable to work, their destiny was extermination.

Mass deportations from the Polish Ghettos to the death Camps were followed by new arrivals from the German Reich. Jews being captured: in France, Italy, Netherlands, Germany, Austria and other European countries.

We should always repeat that the Holocaust was not exclusively a Germanic solution for the 'Jewish Question' but also for homosexuals, handicapped, gypsies and other different people.

By 1945 over three million Polish Jews had been killed and only seventy thousand or less survived.

During the occupation years the Jewish youth waged their war against the Nazis from various partisan units, in the regular Soviet army and in the Polish army. From these three opportunities the Jewish youth of Tarnogrod, and towns near it, had to choose.

When joining the partisans the immediate direction was into the woods. Those who were too young, too old or unable for any reasons chose to hide in a bunker in the forests where a Polish family would hide them for free or for a fee.

In both cases they risked their life because the punishment for helping Jews was death.

Nearly four hundred years before, Tarnogrod was granted the title of royal town in 1567. By 1569 had, as already mentioned, the "privilege" of the "Non Tolerandis Judaeis" which meant its local authorities had the right to forbid Jews to settle or trade in it. This lasted until 1580.

Its population was around fifteen hundred people by 1589.

The town developed rapidly because it was located on the trade route between the Polish cities Lublin and Jaroslaw. Many crafts were being executed and most craftsmen were Jews such as blade smiths, armor smiths, ironmasters, needle makers and goldsmiths. Jews were forbidden in many countries to own land; one simple reason for preferring craftsmanship.

In the second half of the 17st century the town declined because of the invasions of the Tatars (1622 and 1672), the Cossacks of Khmelnitsky and the Swedish-Hungarian army.

Epidemic diseases spread in stages from 1600 till 1722 and also big fires.

These factors contributed to the decline of the town and drop in population. During the Great Northern War (1700-1721) the town was destroyed again. In 1772, Tarnogrod was occupied by the Austrians.

In the 19th century, Poles, Ruthenians and Jews, lived and occupied the city and its surroundings. The town was basically divided between Gentile farmers and Jewish craftsmen and businessmen.

World War I, called the Great War, lasted from 1914 until 1918. This war was considered by historians as the most savage international conflict of mankind. The effect for the Jews was very significant.

There was a very large concentration of Jewish people in the important areas; Austro-Hungary, Russian Empire and German Empire also the enlistment in large numbers in the various fighting armies and the political success of Jewish leaders in influencing political opinions.

About four million Jews lived in the Germanic (Austria-Germany) territories where war was being fought.

Under Russia were six hundred thousand Jews suspected with collaboration (Had family in the other side, spoke a sort of Germanic language called Yiddish, looked too Jewish) were banished from the army.

This caused economical and social problems because these Jewish families impoverished very quickly. Most were deported to the cold Siberian territories of the Russian Empire.

Still about half million Jews wore a Russian military uniform.

On the German side, during World War I, about one hundred thousand Jews served in the German Imperial Army.

Humiliating public declarations were demanded to be signed in the USA and Russia from German Jews; mainly declarations of their patriotism in favor of the country of residence.

History reports indicate that most Jewish leaders had larger sympathy for Germany and the Austro-Hungarian Empire but the historical and documented facts were that Jews fought in the WWI on both sides. Environment was positive enough to allow Zionists organizations in Germany to discuss cooperation over Palestine becoming the Jewish Homeland. Although it sounds weird it is absolutely true.

In spite of occurring small political victories in Germany, Jews were identified with the victors and Germans consoled themselves with the myth about losing due to being "stabbed in the back", that considered Jews traitors.

Also blamed for the Bolshevik´s revolution in Russia, Jews were slaughtered in anti-Jewish Campaigns conducted by the Ukrainians, Russians and Poles. Around one hundred thousand were killed. On this matter Ukrainians had much experience in anti- Jewish Campaigns, Progroms and massacre of defenseless Jews coming from the years 1600s.

Again emigration was the result. When the WWI was over, hundreds of thousands of Jewish people began to leave Europe.

From what we can read about the WWI and the Jews, we get the feeling that regardless of which side they chose to defend, Jews gained a negative status: If on the losers side then they were the main cause of the loss because they acted as traitors. If on the winner side they were only worried about themselves profiteering and being opportunistic.

In the Josef Pilsudsky years, 1926 till 1935, there seemed to be a new opportunity for emancipation for Jews in Poland. But it was not ripe enough and it disintegrated as soon as Pilsudsky, a charismatic popular leader, was gone.

Polish Christian society thought there were too many Jews in Poland. On the other hand the Government was actively helping the Zionist movement in its goal of creating the state of Israel.

Help, seen thru the training and arming of paramilitary Jewish groups, such as Irgun, Haganah and Lehi.

I have been thinking about the word Antisemitism.

Maybe a better word would be Anti-Judaism, was escalating and Catholic oriented trade unions were limiting Jewish participation thru restrictions for government jobs selected only for Catholic poles.

The logical thinking behind this was, less Jews with jobs more non Jews with jobs.

And so, Poland was prepared to lose the WW2, part with the Germans, part with the Soviets and major part with the nationalistic patriotic poles.

Religion in Poland was their strongest asset together with their love for the country. It was small town religious preachers that preached hate ideology (probably due to mental illness of some and extreme fanaticism of others or saying it bluntly because of hate ideology) and thru it, convinced most of the people that their belief was a God given mission and therefore following them was following God.

It is not fair on most Polish people. True!. But who really suffered and paid for the war were the Jewish communities. The last judgment is that sour feeling left after the war in the mouth of those who survived. Many times the comment we heard was "they were worst than the Germans" and that is what prevails. It is a short statement that says much about personal feelings from first level participants and it referred usually to polish Christian people, neighbors.

A Jewish youth that felt Polish, spoke Yiddish and Polish, ready to serve the military and serve his country was frustrated to see that Germans were helped to destroy dreams by their neighbors, colleagues, family and friends. After the WW2 ended with the rendition of Germany, many remaining Jews appeared. Those who survived in the Nazi occupied countries and were hiding all these years; some just hiding; others fighting a guerilla war of attrition; and those who fled Poland into Russia (Soviet Union) and there joined into the war effort.

What should make part of history and therefore taught in schools, in an act of "mea culpa", is the way Poles behaved during and after the WW2, especially those events where public hysteria appeared and the remedy was to kill a Jew.

Result of centuries of preaching, religious education, legal system and church influence, the anti-Jewish character appeared more often than in the past, being used as an excuse for everything unpleasant.

We slowly are learning that ignorant comments made at home by adults, if repeated at school by colleagues and teachers, come back reinforced as truthful.

If then, on Sunday church you have an unfriendly priest delivering a speech full of lies and hatred; your end product is hate transformed into racism and general intolerance, squeezed into a child´s head, and we have produced a future Nazi.

2-THE BRIDE TALES

My name is Roza.

I have been asked to be interviewed about my life during WW2 and answer some questions. What I do not remember, am confused or leave empty gaps, the interviewer will find a way to fill in.

Born April, 1923; in Tarnogrod, Poland. My parents were, Father, Zacharia H.; mother, Hinde Rivque; brother: Majer; sisters: BlIma, Fayga and the youngest: Rachel.

I was born at home; delivered by a Jewish midwife; who happened to be also our neighbor and made some money acting as a matchmaker, a popular activity with Jewish women; at least in those days.

My story I did not write down. Just for being lazy, for the bad feelings caused by most of these memories and for the lack of habit. That is why I am giving this sort of interview. Really a Q&A session. Actually it was a collection of many comments and story-telling, as follows:

Quote ....

-'In general I get a feeling of frustration mixed with anger when I remember or when requested to do so; still, we go ahead with some stories and events just not to leave unanswered some questions I received.

In my family, I had other four half-brothers who were born before us in Poland from my father's first wife, deceased just after WW1; I am one of five children that my mother (second wife to my father) gave birth; four girls and one boy.

From these four half brothers, three migrated to the USA in the early 1920s and established themselves near Chicago. I never met any of them. The fourth brother, Avraham, was in Likew, nearby Tarnogrod, where he had a haberdashery shop and the first Saturday after the invasion had his shop destroyed by the German soldiers.

A friend of him told this story to me:

Avraham had hid in the cellar some valuable goods and merchandises, and a neighbor, a Polish Christian, had denounced him to the SS.

After all the valuables were thrown by the Germans onto the street, he decided to fight the Germans with his hands. The soldiers beat him up furiously and one of them who kicked him in the floor broke his leg. He was older, around 50 years old, he was lucky the Germans did not kill him that day. He survived this event with a badly broken leg and no teeth.

Different luck had my brother Meyer, who was shot dead trying to defend my parents against the German soldiers.

My parents were murdered in front of their house, on that Saturday; the second day after the invasion. They were shot because they did not run to safety when the Germans came and because it was Rosh Hashanah.

Apparently, the German soldiers banged their house's door and after much German insistence my father opened the door and was pushed aside as the soldiers entered; still on the floor my father was ordered by a German officer stand up, go outside the house, stand against the wall and to take off his kippah, the skullcap traditional Jews use on their head, when facing him.

My father ignored the officer's order, meanwhile my family were standing against the wall in the street; then my mother was ordered to take my father's kippah off.

To try to save him, she moved to pick the kippah from his head when my father just nodded to her in a negative way.

With tears in her face she asked the German to forgive her old man. I was told that then my younger brother offered to take the kippah off, and my father nodded negative again by shaking his head.

My mother facing the German soldiers cried for forgiveness. Suddenly my father passed out and fell on the street-walk and my mother and younger brother kneeled down to help him.

The SS officer did not forgive nor hesitate. The three were shot by six soldiers while my mother and brother were trying to assist my father lying on the street floor; in a few moments everything was quiet and silent again. Instantaneous death and my mother desperately crying was the result.

My parents, Zacharia and Hinde Rivque, deeply believed that they were protected by God and whatever happened, it was his will. My father was a religious Jew who kept all Jewish traditions and he came from a religious family of merchants. He had a Jewish beard and peyes; he wore always a kippah and tsitsit.

My mother also came from a religious family of merchants and kept our home strictly kosher; did not wear a wig but wore traditional long dresses and covered her arms.

Father went to Synagogue every morning, every evening and every day he said his prayers wearing his Kippah, Tefillin and Tallit.

As for origin, my parent's families came to Poland from Austria and had accepted, although being religious, that government school was important and sent me and my sisters to public school where we learnt polish, mathematics, history and sang patriotic hymns. I believe the school's name was Szkola Podstawowa im.Marii Curie-Sklodowskiej.

The Polish National anthem was my favorite song. Before classes began, weather permitting, we would sing it daily in the school's patio standing in line by class. After it was finished everybody would patriotically clap.

During the German invasion, my brother Meyer who was murdered by German soldiers, felt under the obligation to stay home and take care of my parents that being old could not survive running into the forest and did not wish to leave their home.

Tarnogrod, was occupied; my sister Bluma was already engaged to Oskar who joined the Partisans and went immediately into hiding in the woods where he left me and my sisters Bluma, Faiga and Rachel to hide in a rural bunker. At the same place were two families from Bilgoraj,various others from Likew and other small towns.

In total, were hidden in this bunker, nearly thirty Jews.

The bunker was full of people and they shared every bit of food. Once, the German soldiers heard the people in the bunker cry and they walked near the bunker's entrance, but did not dare to enter. It smelled so bad and they feared something unknown to be there so they started calling in friendly words for the Jews to come out.

We all in the bunker had to pay monthly for being kept safe from the Germans. In our case it costs us a piece of gold from my bracelet. Polish currency was worthless and nobody accepted it.

The people in the bunker were getting ready to come out. Two brothers, old butchers, were sharpening their butcher's knives. Suddenly in broad daylight, the two brothers started to walk out of the bunker and saw that there were only two German soldiers nearby; so one of them was attacked, with a knife, and badly hurt while the second called aloud for his officer to bring help. The Jews defended themselves not allowing any soldier into the bunker and after three days they gave up.

The older Jews, five of them, were shot outside in the garden. The rest of us remained inside the bunker in silence. The soldiers decided to beat us with their patience.

Their strategy was to wait for us to come out and pick us up one by one. The Germans didn't want to throw bombs into the bunker because they were worried about the Partisans listening to the high noise volume.

But we didn't go out. Anyone not being able to hold his needs was allowed to do them at the farthest corner of the bunker in a hole dug for that purpose about fifty centimeters deep and twenty centimeters wide. A few hours later it was stinking badly, still, nobody complained. In a very low voice some were praying some singing songs for little children that brought comfort; songs that they suddenly remembered.

Before the darkness of the night came down, Oskar, my brother in law, and twelve Partisans appeared and ambushed the Germans killing them all with machine gun fire.

Together with the Partisans were two members of ZEGOTA and another from a Jewish underground group specialized in taking Jews out of Poland and placing in foster homes for Jewish children, in different countries, such as England, USA and Canada.

My sister Rachel was a child and we decided she should be saved.

On that same day she was gone, after a very difficult and highly emotional farewell, but all very conscious that she needed to go. She spent the war years as a daughter of a Polish family in a small rural area near Lublin and we did not know about her until 1957.

In that year when my brother in law, Elia, wrote from Israel saying somebody that seemed to be my younger sister was found in Israel and that she was in a list of survivors with city of origin, Tarnogrod, Poland.

Rachel's foster parents who were University Professors were killed in a bombing of the city of Lublin. After two days without any news, a partisan group went to the rural house where she lived and took her with them and left her with a senior sister of a nun's convent. She and other five girls were there waiting for a means of transport out of Europe.

All six girls were Jewish and as soon as WW2 was finished some people from ZEGOTA picked them up. ZEGOTA was an organization created by two Christian Polish women with the purpose of saving Jews from extermination in Poland.

They collected Jewish people in need of protection and organized ways to give them a home and/ or find a way to smuggle them out of Poland. They cared and did a tremendously brave job.

They were told they would migrate to Israel (or Mandate Palestine as was called in those days). From 1945 until 1948 illegal immigration was the largest method of immigration to Israel, because the British prohibited legal migration under the mandate they received from the United Nations.

There was the case of a vessel coming from Russia.

The vessel was called Norsyd/Hagana and sailed from La Spezia, on the Italian coast down the Adriatic Sea, with more than 2.670 passengers giving notice to the British that despite obstacles, Jewish migration, although considered illegal, would continue.

Like other vessels, the Norsyd/Hagana was detected by the British near Port Said, In Egypt; boarded by the troops of two British destroyers and sent to Cyprus. Most adults on the vessel were Betarites, members of right wing Jewish Political party called Betar, and some had undergone basic army training as Partisans or members of the Russian or Polish armies. One night, after four weeks in Cyprus, the captain of the vessel and the crew managed to slip out of the British control and under the cover of darkness, it started a five day journey along the eastern shores of the Mediterranean Sea until it reached Tel Aviv.

In the last hours before arriving in Israel, the vessel was escorted by the organization called Irgun, whose task included the logistics of disembarkation onto Israeli shores and disappearance by mixing into the local community.

While in Tel Aviv waters, a British vessel approached and boarded it. Most immigrants, directed by Irgun members, jumped into the sea and began to swim ashore, despite firing from the British.

Once ashore they mixed with local people taking a sun bath and most disappeared from the sight of the British soldiers.

To be safe, the locals had been coached to receive the immigrants and supply them with a set of shorts and t-shirts.

Rachel was one of the swimmers. She was guided by an Irgun female member off the beach just with her clothes and a small laundry sack. She was directed to a Kibbutz with other children of a similar background and disappeared in the Kibbutz.

She had to enter Israel illegally; there was no other way for an orphan with no known family or friends in Israel. It was July 1946. This vessel was in the Aliyah Bet Ships program.

In fact the British established that there was an eighteen thousand people quota, which was very low indeed. More than sixty illegal immigration sailings were scheduled during these years but just a few were able to make it to shore.

American sector Camps did not impose restrictions on leaving the Camps; normally they and their counterparts in the French and Italian armies turned a blind eye on these movements.

On the other hand the British were strongly opposed to the outgoing movement and imposed an armed naval blockade to prevent Jews landing in Mandate Palestine. Those caught attempting to enter illegally were stopped and some sent to internment Camps in Cyprus, Palestine and Mauritius.

The British held as many as fifty thousand Jewish prisoners in these Camps. British methods got worldwide attention thru the incident of the Exodus; the ship was intercepted, attacked, and boarded by Britain´s naval forces, diverted back to Europe and after resistance from its passengers, the displaced persons and Holocaust survivors on the vessel were again back in Germany.

My husband Majer went, in 1957, to Israel and there confirmed that Rachel was my younger sister and she told him the story about travelling from Europe to Israel as an orphan after the WW2 had ended.

Going back to the first subject," Life in the Bunker".

Except three elderly people that did not make it thru the first winter in the bunker, the rest survived until the end of WW2.

About those who died, I always had the feeling that they were not sick people; their death occurred out of deep disappointment and sadness. There was plenty time for thinking, for speculating, for meditation and for disappointment. In this psychological cocktail we ought to include disillusion with our dreams.

They always spoke of Poland, the mother country, abandoning them so easily and effortless in the hands of the Nazis. These three old Jews had served in the Polish Army, two as corporals and the third cleaning horse manure in the stables.

Still they were proud to have served and now very sad after losing everything. Their whereabouts, hidden goods, mainly books, were informed to the SS by ex colleagues from the Army days.

I think they died of sadness. It is a sadness that touches religion, depressive, disappointing, frustrating, in search of support; kills all hope and leaves no future. Still most people that experience this sadness are able to survive, build a future and recover partially (or totally) the will to live.

And the war went on and us witnessing some humans, rather a lot of them, behaving like animals. In the bunker, thru the employees of the farm, we received news from what was occurring in the cities and what went on with the Partisan we knew.

After nearly one year hiding in the bunker we needed to change our hiding location. The Partisans had recommended this action. This new place was also a farm at about two hundred kilometers from our first bunker.

We walked and got lifts on friendly farmer's trucks; it took us about three days.

In our second hideaway we were nine Jews. It was also a bunker but excavated in the ground floor of a barn where we co-habited with horses, dogs, pigs and goats.

The hole in the ground was one and a half meters deep, four meters wide and five meters long. The top were two removable parts wider than the bunker. When closed we kneeled or sat on the excavated floor. On top of us the two wooden tops covered with dry grass. On top of these tops a few pigs and chickens.

Hidden, when the farmer or his wife told us to do so, we were so uncomfortable because inside the bunker it was necessary to kneel, lie down or sit on the humid floor.

Every time there was a 'Germans are coming' alarm we run into the hole and kneeled down; sometimes during ten or twenty minutes, sometimes lasted for hours. Like when the inspection troops came after lunch and had a rest in the barn for two or three hours. My knees hurt for hours after we got out from the bunker and part of my legs were numb.

This bunker belonged to a farm located in between the towns of Modliborzyce and Ordynack in the Lublin district and frequented by the Partisan group of Avraham Bron, one of the few Jews that served in the Polish Army as a Corporal before the German's invasion.

We paid for our safety and worked for our food doing activities that the farmer requested. Paid with golden pieces taken from gold bracelets, earrings or necklaces and our guarantee were the partisan that periodically came from the woods to see us, to eat and rest.

If anyone of us would be missing or in the hands of the Germans, there was to be a partisan judgment immediately and if anyone found guilty he would be sentenced to death with no delay.

One evening, after having dinner, the Partisan group heard and monitored a group of six German soldiers in a surprise visit. The Partisans hid themselves in the bunker, on top of a few trees and inside the barn.

The security sign was to sing like an owl. So when some soldiers were coming in and passed any of the Partisans, the partisan would sing like an owl informing where they were and that he walked in the direction of the barn. The soldiers were approaching silently the barn, two from behind and four divided into two left of the door and two on the right.

The two Partisans sitting each on top of a tree with many branches and leaves were now positioned behind the Germans.

Four Germans with their backs against us.

The other two had already reached the back of the barn and would try to enter thru a window. One helped the other get up to this window and slide into the barn. As soon as he touched the ground, his neck was sliced and his head lay separated from the body in the darkness of the back of the barn.

The other soldier could not reach the window by himself so he looked for something like a stool or chair which he found in a few minutes.

The soldiers in the front waited for the shooting to begin at the back of the barn. The second soldier placed the stool near the window and got up on it. In a few seconds he was already squeezing himself thru the window and when he had half of his body thru, he was shot in the head.

This shot signaled to the Partisans on the trees that the soldiers needed to be killed immediately and both started shooting. The four soldiers died in a very short time.

The Partisans prepared to hide these corpses in a common burial hole with their clothes and rifles. The guns and ammunition were kept. After they finished the clean up the chief of the Partisans gave an order in Yiddish and all went away wishing us a good night.

My sister Bluma got closer to one of them and whispered some words to which he nodded with his head and later kissed her in the cheek.

I knew what it was. A verbal message to her husband Oskar who was in the woods and was one of the leaders of his Partisan group.

Oskar was having headaches and did not have drugs for his diabetes but on the rest everything was working. These Partisans were from a Jewish brigade.

They were getting ready to coordinate their war efforts with the Red Army. Although there were other Jewish brigades within the Polish army some of the Partisan leaders preferred Russian officers than Polish.

During three years they burnt German Officer's quarters, they killed German drunks at night near the whorehouses, attacked small farms that were too friendly with the German soldiers, bombed trucks transporting goods and foodstuff for the German Army and in general killing as many soldiers as possible.

They received news from the Ghettos, the transportation facilities, labor Camps and from the extermination Camps.

The Partisan leaders had access to intelligence information and terrible news continued to arrive.

The news was about the misbehavior of civilians, soldiers and even some Partisans with Jewish Polish people. Many of them, quite visibly, collaborated fully with the Germans. Some Jewish people were hidden by neighbors in their houses.

A third neighbor informed the German SS; another was hidden by the priest inside a church and after the Germans were informed both were shot dead; an old couple of Jews with two grandchildren were hiding in a bakery; somebody close informed and they were all shot trying to escape.

During all the WW2 we were protected by the Partisans and were hidden in bunkers in farms near the woods until the good news arrived.

We survived but the taste was bitter. I still feel the pain in my knees. The physical pain of injury and I also feel the pain in my heart for my parents, brother, friends and neighbors murdered by hatred lovers whose souls I hope get rotten in hell.

Such a highly educated people with a pragmatic and gentleman's behavior to become blood thirsty animals when guided by men with a hellish vision, was unbelievable. How was it possible?'

Unquote ……………………………………………

Following comments are from interviewer:

Inside the pockets of used clothes, in need of a wash, I found a written comment on a small card that I wrote sometime in the past:

"Hidden hate, inbuilt in the DNA of some people by the transformation of feelings belonging to the dark ages of mankind, mixed with ideas washed in the brains of children studying religion with prejudices for centuries, did come out and showed itself. Its real name could be anti-Judaism but it is intolerance."

First in the wild compulsory conversions, followed by the Crusades, then during methodical Inquisition and expulsion from Spain and Portugal, and then improved and more effective in the Holocaust years during WW2.

Between this major anti-Jewish events acts of hatred occurred ad Jewish people were killed for multiple reasons.

It will not go away and disappear as many wish. It will stay to remind us of our animal origins, our primitive conditions of Hate, Fear, Hunger and Need of Sex; and our acquired lack of tolerance and wish to understand. It feeds on hatred and the antidote is education at home and at school.

The spark can be anything, even fear, or a self-caused harm. In most places there was fuel in the air and they were eager and ready to set up a fire.

Education of what?

Of Tolerance, of diversity and in general of respect for differences.'

This interview was really conducted at four hands where I accepted some of the interviewer's opinion's as if they were mine surpassing in this manner my barriers in expressing myself.

UNQUOTE ………………

3-THE GROOM`S STORIES

My name is Majer.

I was asked to answer some questions and to comment some events of my youth in Poland that means until 1939; all this in years of small talk.

On September of that year we escaped from the German soldiers that invaded Poland and started the WW2.

I tell these stories and events just to answer questions placed before me. Basically I don't want to comment because it upsets me deeply and I internalize this feeling. Normally I avoid unpleasant themes and this is for sure one of them. Also because of my personal relationship with the interviewer whom I know for a long time.

In other chapters we deal with details and stories of Majer: arrival in Russia;into the army;out of the army;end of the war, DR Camps and direction to thr New World.

QUOTE ....

-'I was born in Tarnogrod, Poland; on June, 1st, 1918.

My son, in various opportunities made questions about my youth and the WW2 which I sort of answered in parts and pieces. Let him complete the empty spaces.

I am telling my story since being a baby till the German invasion of Poland. A period of twenty one years that I spent in Poland. I am focused in showing my story in parallel against history, as I have been told and read.

In the Jewish section of my town, Tarnogrod, we also had our local Polish heroes. In our school they taught us about them. I am not sure if that was extra curricula or standard Ministry of Education.

Josef Pilsudski, was a local and national hero back from WW1, in jail since June, 1917 and there was a lot of political pressure by most central European countries to free him. A few months later, in November, 1918 ; Germany surrendered and Poland was presented with access to the sea. World War One ended.

-'I was delivered at home on June, 1st, 1918.

A home birth, where the midwife was one of the neighbors, Jewish, married to the butcher who was a good friend of my father.

The midwife was also a permanent member of the Camp's gossip committee and well-known local matchmaker.'

-'My family consisted of my father, Guedalia and my mother, Szjandla, and my brothers, Haim and Wolf. After my birth, nearly three years later, was born our youngest brother, Elia.

-'So this was my family. We were very simple people and not poor. My father was a craftsman, a tailor and my mother took care of the house, the food and the children.

Until seven years old I played nearly all day in our bedroom when cold and outside our home when it was warm. I never felt very warm.

Our toys were made of wood; a horse, a truck and a duck. Frequently made by my father.

One of our neighbors had a ball made of cloth and sometimes he would play with us. We did not have a sister so we needed to help my mother every day with small house chores, such as cleaning, washing and helping serve the table and make the beds.

My brothers Wolf and Haim already attended school, the 'Yiddish Cheder ' in the afternoon and the 'Goyishe' school in the morning from 8 till 12 a.m.

It is 1925 and I am going to start next September and learn the Polish National Song, to write and read in Polish language and the numbers.

Wolf and Haim already knew. They counted without limits, wrote letters and copied stories.

My parents always talked to us after dinner, before we were sent to bed, and whispered between themselves other subjects afterwards. While we were present and still sitting at the table the conversation run on what was done that day at school, sing a song and what have we learnt in 'cheder' that day.

Then, a short Q&A session, about everything that was going on at the Jewish school, and at the Gentile school.

Sometimes we had a chance of asking my father what he did and what his plans were.

Normally he told us his plans in the form of dreams where we always ended up in the USA. More specifically in New York in a suburb called Brooklyn.

Some nights after having a chat with my brothers I also dreamt with the USA, with having a new house, a big car and tall buildings. Everything was my father`s description!

My father's job was that of a handyman, especially wood repairs and wooden furniture. He planned to build a factory of wooden artifacts such as tables, chairs, doors and windows; with many workers. I also wanted to work with wood; in the United States of America. To be rich and travel, to see the world.

-' And to go to Israel and see Jerusalem' - my mother would normally suggest.

Life was calm and friendly although everything limited as were our resources. Sometimes at Jewish school we would hear that the night before some drunkards came into the Jewish sector swearing and hitting anyone walking by and usually started a fire in a barn or wooden deposit.

The drunkards were insulting the Jews, screaming into the night that Jews kill children and drink their blood in ritual ceremonies, accusation known as blood libel; that Jews murdered God, called Deicide; that they were traitors and other insults; then threw a few stones and go.

At school we asked our teacher, and he refused to talk too much about it and ignored our questions about, the truthfulness and the reasons of the insults.

At home, at night sitting at the table for dinner, sometimes I would tell what I heard and ask my older brothers for an explanation which they did not have, except that they heard that in Germany there was a political party called National Socialist Party, called the Nazi Party, that was promising to get rid of Jews, gypsies and homosexuals.

They went one step higher than the inquisition. The Nazis wanted to eliminate completely the Jewish people while the inquisition mainly was worried about expelling the Jews from their land or convert.

To eliminate sounded strange to Portuguese and Spanish.

Still, although not their main target, they did burn at the stake thousands in Spain, Portugal and some colonies like Mexico. It sounded strange, probably inhuman and criminal; I repeat.

Maybe some of these Germans come to Poland?

My mother was always nervous when the subject was problems for the Jews, Germans, drunkards, fights, brawls and similar. My father scratched his beard and shook his head in disbelief.

Always the answer was that we are Jews, thanks God!, and we needed to follow the teachings of the Rabbis and practice the commandments or good deeds, called Mitzvot, and that God will always protect us and decide our futures.

Thru ritual circumcision on every male baby we registered in the alliance with God.

My brothers always mentioned we should go to Israel our future homeland, where everybody was peaceful and where the land belonged to the Jews. I had heard of other people in Israel but never considered it an issue for me.

These people were in the story of Abraham, Sara, Agar and Ismael and the invasion of Alexander and the resistance of the Maccabean. So apart from these people the rest were absolutely Jewish. Few drunkards, No Nazis.

At fifteen my father took me to Warsaw to see what a wood products factory looked like. Before he had taken Wolf and Haim to a Taylor shop in Warsaw and they lived there Sunday evening till Friday noon in a sweathouse where they learned the Tailor trade and earned a few "kopeks" which they brought home to my mother after paying in Warsaw for the rent, food and weekend transport.

For us clothes were manufactured 'at home" by my mother and my father, who bought the cloth, buttons, needles and other accessories.

My father introduced me to the wood products factory's manager. A middle-aged man, with blue eyes and a black short beard. The man called Theodor (In honor of Theodor Herzl, he explained for quite some time the Zionist movement, Herzl's vision) explained all sections of the factory to me and the learning schedule, the pay per week, where to eat and where to sleep.

In the whole factory there were thirty five employees.

The owner was a rich Jew, originally from Spain, whose family had migrated during inquisition to Morocco and from there to southern France, Austria and finally Poland ; who had other business in Warsaw and came to visit the factory once a week.

When I saw him the first time, I said to myself, I want to be like him. But if asked by my parents I would say that I wanted to be like my father. Still I was never sure what exactly he did for a living.

When we learnt that during Rosh Hashanah, on September 1st, 1939; that German troops had invaded Poland in an agreement with the Soviet Union and divided between them the country, we decided with my brothers to leave Tarnogrod immediately.

My father was sick then but decided with my mother to join us in our journey to Russia.

We left that evening together with four other Jewish neighbors in the same direction and for the same reason: to survive.

We already had heard of the 'Kristallnacht' and other events in Nazi Germany that occurred in the last few years and the growing violence against Jews in Germany and also in Polish towns with German origin majority and we knew we would be killed if remained in our birth town, Tarnogrod.

We had heard many stories about the SA, the SS troops and the Nazi Party and were worried but the majority of the stories were dismissed as invention or exaggeration.

After nearly three days walk we arrived in Russia and were met there by members of the 1st Polish army and invited to join the army and fight against the Nazis. My father got worst and we found a room to rent with a Polish peasant, inside Poland but very close to the Russian border and left my parents with him. We paid the rent one year in advance.

But why did we leave my parents and brother Elia at the Polish side of the border?

Because the Russian authorities would only accept them, my elderly parents, sick father and child brother; if they worked for the army. As they could not do any hard work they were expelled from Russia back to Poland and here comes the story of the Polish peasant and his bunker.

We joined the armies. Suggested by my father, Wolf joined the 1st Polish Army and started training next day.

Haim and I finally joined the Red Army. It took everything valuable to bribe the guards and the political representative on our regiment.

The 1st Byelorussian Front was a giant complex of armies and had a section for new recruits without any training. Elia was to be together with my parents until things changed and/or be of age.

There was daily training in the fields. Sometimes, with dummies for target shooting, other times running away from the German troops.

My father was happy with what he had and considered that he had three of his children working as trainees, a prince's dream.

For nearly three months until the end of 1939 we were trained in the basics of military life: marching, shooting, eating, sleep, march, shoot, eat, sleep and so on. Once or twice a week there were political classes which I recall like a brainwashing effort from the Russian political coordinators.

We were considered second class soldiers for being Polish and Jews. Our dear Russian military colleagues would normally call us the 'Rabbi brigade'.

In spite of the political classes and their efforts to convince us of the niceties of their ideology we never became even sympathizers of the Soviets and their communist party.

In our brigade there were many Jews but it was not exclusively made of Jews. About ten or fifteen percent were Jews from various nationalities.

I and my brothers made plans for after the war. We all had defined a destination: United States of America. Many Jews from Poland had gone there and all send letters informing that they either are, or were going to be, millionaires.

Nevertheless, whenever some non-family person would inquire of our after the war plans, we would always answer: the Holy Land of Israel.

The big question was if we would be accepted as migrants in the USA.

Although the political classes explained, tried to brainwash and affirmed that the enemy of the working classes was the bourgeoisie, especially the Americans, we still considered that the USA would be the best place to live.

In Tarnogrod there were many families that had already a relative living there and it was considered that Polish people were welcome.

But there was a doubt in the air. The war in Europe started and the British already said they had a commitment to protect Poland from any foreign aggression; but nothing coming from the United States of America's side.

Until the end of 1939 we stayed stationed in the border between Poland and Germany. Then we went back and forward between Poland and the borders of Germany and Russia. This lasted about one year.

February 1941 we were ordered to march back into the heart of the Soviet Union. It was a very difficult march, in the middle of winter, snowing most of the time and very cold.

After two weeks we arrived outside of Moscow and set Camp there.

Germany had invaded Poland, France, Denmark, Norway, Belgium and The Netherlands and, although they had an agreement with Russia, people said it was preparing to invade Russia. Which they did in 1941; the non-aggression pact between Hitler and Stalin was thrown into the garbage bin.

Germany decided to invade Russia in June, 1941.

We were a long period stationed near Moscow until we were re-arranged and our unit became part of the big Red Army that went after Nazi Germany.

Our orders were to avoid taking prisoners and if in doubt shoot him dead'

This was the hour that Hitler dreamt himself in Napoleon footsteps but the Russian would give everything to keep this victory in their imaginary empire.

We were Red Army soldiers and weather our division was after Hitler or Red Army defending Moscow we were trained to believe and act as winners and the best;

Thousands of prisoners were gathered in Camps in spite of our instructions: wherever we went we were putting soviets and some polish in Camps. One evening I met my two brothers and we agreed to pass to the American side when the right opportunity arose.

By our officer planning we would be near Munchen in two weeks. Some Jews, from Lublin, serving in a division stationed nearby in the forest were discussing to abandon the Russian uniform and join the American occupied zone as a first step to migrating to the USA. Each of us speculated where to go: USA, Israel (although still called Palestine by nearly everybody), Argentina and Canada. My brother Haim made an acid comment about needing lots of money to enter a rich country.

After some cigarettes my two brothers in Russian uniform decided that after conquering German headquarters the direction to follow was the Holy Land, Israel.

I also agreed but in principle.

UNQUOTE ……..……………

The following are comments by the interviewer:

It feels good to be a winner but unfortunately you cannot do it all the time.

Although there was a contradiction in all Jews, the remaining of course could feel winners of WW2. Where there was a killing machine installed to exterminate completely, without a doubt all the people of the Bible it so happened that the Nazis could not finish what they started. The main reasons are because of the English and the Americans.

The Americans had to be pushed insistently by that great man, Sir Winston Churchill but the honor of bringing them to the fighting belongs to this single person who, they say, disliked Jews

Now the English fought their own war by sea and from the air, had their Dunkirk until physical and mental exhaustion and tried to ignore war.

Thanks to Churchill the British Empire convinced the upcoming American empire to join the war and with this won it.

I just wanted to register and express the gratitude of millions to the American and the English people for saving us but specially to Mr. Churchill, normally these days in a more spiritual environment he would be chosen to be the Messiah and King of Israel.

My father was not very keen to talk about this period of his life. A bit upset about stories in Poland and annoyed with the events in the Russian army. But he was thankful to a few.

4-BUNKER & PARTISANS

In the bunker life was horrible. So it was hard to get Roza to continue the interview and below we reproduce an edited version:

Quote …

But we wanted to survive. It was more than 'I want' it was 'I need to". We had hoped for a better life. A life we could have enjoyed happy moments with others. The survival instinct was strong and active.

We paid rental fees to stay in the bunker and not all moments were safe and quiet in the rural areas we stayed.

A memory that kept appearing, was that of Mrs. Guideman and her little baby. The baby had maybe six months old.

One of the persons renting space in the bunker was this mother and her baby daughter. Nobody heard or saw Mr. Guideman; that was her name or the name she was known between us.

She was quite nervous, always with red humid eyes that seemed to have been crying for all of humanity; always in a dark spot or in a corner, never said hullo or good day. Sometimes she would mumble a 'sorry' when bumping into someone. She did not speak except the possible minimum number of words. She just nodded with her head as an answer to everything.

Knew nobody and was not known by anybody.

Some elderly ladies speculated about Mrs. Guideman being Jewish. She was normally invisible, talking to herself and getting very nervous when the baby started crying. Never let anybody in the bunker hold the baby or even speak baby nonsense.

One day, the baby from Ruth Guideman started to cry loudly. She yelled apparently in pain. Most probably she was hungry, in pain or uncomfortable or a mix of all.

Her mother didn´t, apparently, register the baby´s signals and whenever the baby screamed she tried first breast feeding, if it didn´t work she tried singing by mumbling something we couldn´t understand, or checking if her nappy was wet or full or walking around the room shaking the baby and speaking softly to her. Always very nervous when German patrols were announced.

Next few minutes we were informed that the German´s patrol was nearby; the baby´s mother tried various methods of calming down the baby girl.

Every second Mrs. Guideman grew more desperate because her daughter would not stop screaming and we all thought we could hear the German soldier´s boots as they got closer and closer.

The SS Patrol did not seem to care or maybe they were sure there were no enemies in this part of the forest and the group of soldiers walked and talked, smoked a cigarette and laughed at some jokes or funny comments.

The baby sobbed and tried to scream. In an instant the baby was silent. We could hear the noise of the boots and the soldiers, the feared SS troops, talking amenities. They kept on coming up to the main house.

The barn was locked.

The SS soldiers, as a routine, would walk around the bunker located in the barn, felt the bad smell, commented about it, turned around and walked away slowly; laughing about some funny comment made by one of them.

In a few seconds they were away from the area of the bunker and back to the army truck. There was a deep silence for a few seconds that appeared to last an eternity.

Mrs. Guideman had managed to keep her baby silent and the bunker neighbors were relieved that the Germans had walked away and no hassle occurred.

A few minutes later a loud scream came from the furthest part inside the bunker. It was Mrs.Guideman open heart screaming that felt as if someone was having a leg amputated with no anesthetic. It was her!

She had unwillingly suffocated her child. Mrs. Guideman was with the dead child's body in her arms and talked to her baby as if she did not recognize she was dead. She cried and talked to the baby. Tears came out from everywhere in her face.

Talked and cried and endless mumbling, her eyes popping out and her face colored red. Tears kept pouring from her eyes.

She talked softly and cuddled the dead baby; cried in silence a few minutes until abruptly started to scream louder and louder. In a few minutes she silenced.

Suddenly she bent down and left the static lifeless body on the ground and started screaming and walking on her knees in de bunker, into the dark and threw herself into the accumulated excrements screaming 'my baby, my baby'.

Two or three women took care of her and other ladies washed and cleaned the baby. An older man prayed and delivered the baby's soul to God.

The baby was buried far away from the bunker, far away from the farm under a large tree; in the woods surrounded by big trees. All of us got our shirts cut as if we were her close family.

The casket, that really was a wooden box, was lowered into a hole dug beneath a tree and the older Jew recited the psalms and read the corresponding scriptures. After the casket was lowered everybody, recited Kaddish, that is, praises to God.

The mourning period (shiva) was seven days as tradition requests and (Shloshim) thirty days after the date of burial.

The next seven days we sat in mourning all who remained in the bunker and Mrs. Guideman cried in silence and chose to stay alone avoiding speaking with the others. She was destroyed and deeply depressed. She was not interested in empty chats and whatever spoken to her she mumbled back:

-'Nothing will bring her back'.

The day after Shiva she jumped into a river; on a rainy day. The river was about half a kilometer from the farm. She cried until she met her baby again a week after her passing away. Nobody ever heard anything about her family or her husband. She and the baby were left at the bunker by her brother who joined the local freedom fighters or guerilla as they were starting to be kown.

Life had to go on; I suffered from pain in my knees.

Like when the Partisan's inspection troops came after lunch and had a rest in the barn for two or three hours. My knees hurt for hours after we got out from the bunker and part of my legs were numb.

This bunker belonged to a farm located in between the towns of Modliborzyce and Ordynack, in the Lublin district, and frequented by the Partisan group of Avraham Bron, one of the few Jews that served in the Polish Army as a Corporal before the German's invasion.

This group was very active in fighting the Germans, destroying their supplies and finding places to hide Jews and others persecuted by the Nazis.

If anyone of us would be missing or in the hands of the Germans, there was to be a partisan judgment immediately and if found guilty sentenced with no delay.

As the Partisans appeared from time to time, Bluma used to get information about Oskar. He was having headaches and did not have drugs for the control of his diabetes but on the rest everything was working.

These Partisans were from a Jewish brigade. They were getting ready to coordinate their war efforts with the Red Army.

Although there was other Jewish brigades within the Polish army some of the partisan leaders preferred Russian officers, of course after Russia and Germany cancelled their non aggression agreement.

During three years the Partisans burnt German Officer's quarters, they killed German soldiers that were drunk at night near the whorehouses near the red lamp districts, attacked small farms that were too friendly with the German soldiers, ambushed small transports, planted bombs in bars frequented by the Nazis ; in general killed as many Nazi soldiers as possible.

They received news from the Ghettos, the transportation and forced labor Camps and from the extermination Camps.

The Partisan leaders had access to intelligence information and terrible news did arrive.

The news was about the behavior of civilians, soldiers and even some Partisans. Many of them, quite visibly, collaborated fully with the Germans. For opportunistic reasons, for ideological motivation or survival instinct or for some other reasons, they collaborated and participated with the murder of thousands or millions of human beings.

Historians register that Poland unlike other countries in Europe was no official collaborator. Be it at economical or Political level. Poland occupied by the Germans had the largest resistance movement in occupied Europe.

The Polish army fought underground and in the forests the Partisans.

Polish citizens that were known as collaborators were the German minority living in Pomerania and

Western Silesia. Statistics show that during the WW2 about three million polish citizens of German origin signed the 'Volksdeutsche' official list.

For the Polish underground these signees committed high treason according to their law. Numbers indicate that there were considered "Polish collaborators" a few hundred thousand Poles within a population of thirty five millions.

When a Pole declared being 'Volkdeutsche' it meant he considered his German ethnicity. Also, as collaborators, were considered the Blue Police although some acted as spies for the partisan, disobeyed German orders and some helped the Jews.

Antisemitism was probably the reason why Partisan (Jewish versus Non Jewish) clashed and some members of the Non Jewish Partisan groups were collaborators of the Nazis. They basically acted as informers. The damage to be caused to Jews was their target.

The most complicated example of human behavior was the Jewish Ghetto Police. Polish Jews who could be relied upon to follow and obey German orders. The apparent cruelty coming from these was enormous.

Some were mean persons, others just did not have a choice and they functioned with double standards. They followed Nazi orders but sometimes also used their position to hide and save lives.

They were considered collaborators regardless of their good actions and destiny reserved a strange place for their future. If they did not accept their functions they run into deep problems and were punished and often eliminated.

An important damage to Jews was the well organized list which Jewish organizations that kept their names, children, address and general information such as professional activities. This information in the hands of the Gestapo and SS had an enormous negative impact on Jewish lives.

Having written the opinions of others we make a point in trying to understand Roza`s comments about her fellow Polish people being 'of worst behavior' than the German Forces. Worst, in this case, meant against Jews with rage and with the intention to eliminate.

The final solution to the Jewish Question.

They lived to make the Jewish people disappear from earth.

Brutality, force and hate made part of their inner self.

What surprised, and therefore caused more pain, was that school friends, neighbors you played ball with, people you worked with and did business with; many became openly Anti-Semitic and were seen collaborating with the Germans, not to deliver any material goods or wealth, or secrets or military know-how, but to send them to the extermination Camps and have their homes looted and robbed of any valuables.

You played and worked together and next day they delivered you to the Nazis in a tray for feeding their gods in an unclear public sacrifice.

It could be possible to opt for treason if you are afraid or in danger but many took this collaborating attitude for ambition and for hate. Hate of all difference being it black, gipsy or Jew.

Maybe for revenge. But revenge for what reason?

Recognized by most people, the Polish were brave and resisted well over their means the efforts of the Germans to conquer and dominate, but they were anti-Jewish and for no reason, except hate culture.

Their love and hate affair was satisfied when the undesirable races,such as Jews, Blacks,Gypsies, and other considered lower ethnicities would be cleansed. Not segregated or separated, but eliminated.

In the Middle Ages to solve an enormous problem with the other children (except the first born child who inherited nearly everything).

To avoid fraternal wars, the nobility and priesthood created the Crusades with a fantastic marketing project:

-A Christian worldwide effort -Mostly with nobility as leaders; to come back from Jerusalem alive and having fought the non-believers and probably won some land rights and brought some relics from the Holy Land. -A fanatic group of priests to warm up the troops with idealism and hatred -An interesting enemy: the keepers of sacred places and Jerusalem (original Christian sects, original Jewish sects,Islamic groups and others) -The promise of right to the land even kingdoms to some -The chance to be far away from Europe's wars -Men's only Clubs (The Orders: Templar, Hospitaliers and others).

This was the soup that brought together parts and pieces and brew antisemitism. Intolerance, as a general approach; intolerance, that until this day has specialized in segregating by sex, by color, by race, by religion, by size and other references.

Psychological scientists have identified in our dark parts of the brain four basic characteristics considered prime sources of life, such as; Sex, Hunger, Hate and Fear. By using these sources it can be built an enormous list of personalities. We have not tamed these characteristics yet. Considering education, which is acquired and social pressures, we will have peaceful societies when conditions are ripe for it.

Unquote …………

5- IN THE ARMY

Continuation of Majer's interviews …

I, Majer and my brothers, Wolf, Haim and Elia left our home together with our sick mother, Szjandla, and thru an organization specialized in protecting Jews paid to a polish peasant to keep her and other elderly people hidden in the forest. Normally peasants would build a bunker to store things and foods for winter months. This bunker was a continuation at the end of the barn and sometimes had a connection between the main house and it.

We, the brothers, decided that Elia, the youngest brother with nearly twelve years old would remain with our mother, hidden in the forest in a bunker, while we fled to Russia and try to join the 1st Polish Army or the 1BF (First Bielorussian front).

I decided to write down the important news from our day-to-day in a small copybook with black covers and nearly fifty white clean pages.

The idea of writing down every day was to have a written witness for our lives. The surprising thing is that few writings are available from my days of youth. Most were never written, many were destroyed and lost.

If I only knew before what was going to be with my life I surely would have had the discipline to write things down.

Again, we and many other Jewish people, were helped by ZEGOTA (Zydowska Organizajca Bojowa-ZOB) and after some time hiding in various Camps we were delivered to the 1st Polish Army.

This Polish Army joined the Russian 1st Bielorussian Front (1BF) and participated in many successful military operations. The officers of the 1st Polish Army asked the Russians to keep in the Russian Army the Polish Jews.

The main reason, and this they did not tell the Russians; was that the Jews, although Polish, were suspected to be traitors and collaborate with the Germans because, according to their internal talks; they spoke Yiddish, a Germanic language. The Russians asked their commissar, who was a Jew himself, who dismissed the idea of Jewish spies for the Germans.

ZEGOTA was a Christian charity organization that was the continuation of a secret project set up solely for the purpose of giving aid to Jews, founded in 1942 by Zofia Kossak-Szczucka and Wanda Krahelska-Filipowicz. Members of the Polish Undergound that had contacts with secret organizations. Originally, when founded in 1942, it was composed of Jews and Non-Jews. It was specialized in saving Jewish children by taking them into convents, orphanages and foster homes.

ZEGOTA primary purpose was to provide social welfare, such as money, housing, and medical aid.

Back to the army.

In February 1944 we went for the Dnieper-Carpathian Offensive and still in February we started the Rogachev-Zhlobin Operation.

Next activities were Brobruisk Offensive where the 1st Bielorussian Front (1st BF) trapped forty thousand

German troops; the Lublin-Brest Offensive was next in summer and in the months of August and September the 1BF engaged in cleaning out Germans operations to the east of the Vistula River.

During this cleaning of Germans occurred the Battle of Radzymin.

Later on in September 1BF forces with the 1st Polish Army in front captured a suburb (Praga) of Warsaw.

And the brothers were back in Poland! After so much effort to flee to any faraway place they were back.

At the beginning of 1945 the forces of the 1BF, as part of the Vistula-Poznan Operation which was part of the Vistula-Oder offensive, performed the attack named Warsaw-Poznan Operation and afterwards began the offensive towards Pillkallen, in East Prussia, where they met the tough 3rd Panzer Army of the Germans.

On January, 24th, the 1BF and 2BF attacked Pomerania. Germany's 2nd Army was cut off.

After very hard fighting on January, 25th, the 1BF cut off the city of Poznan and took sixty six thousand Germans prisoners.

1BF, on Jan, 31st, reaches river Oder and establishes a bridgehead less than sixty kilometers from Berlin. On the first two days of February the 1BF surrounds the town of Kustrin and reaches south of Frankfurt.

The high command ordered the 8th Guards Army to lay siege to the city which gave up on February, 23rd; and the rest of the 1BF continued its eighty kilometers a day advance. Warsaw was near.

Marshall Zhukov was appointed commander of the 1BF, in November 1944, with the sole purpose of capturing Berlin. Before, were captured Poland and East Prussia.

In March 27, 28, 29 and 30 the 1BF took Danzig and Kustrin after thirty days siege.

In April,1945, General Zhukov concentrated the military forces of the 1BF in front of Seelow Heights.

By then the 2BF moved into the area just left by the 1BF.The operation to take Seelow heights started with assault by the 1st Ukrainian front who found great difficulties in getting thru German defensive lines but after hitting hard for three days they went thru and started forcing their way approaching Berlin suburbs.

A battle of attrition continued for the position of Seelow heights. On the next day German defenses were penetrated by Russian forces that moved fast to encircle Berlin.

On April 22nd the northern and eastern suburbs of Berlin had been penetrated by soviet armies. An encirclement operation between 1BF and 1UF was finished and a house to house fighting started.

A few days later, units of 1BF meet west of Berlin. The city was now completely encircled by eight Russian armies and General Zhukov refused to grant an armistice and demanded unconditional surrender.

The German commander General Weidling surrendered to General Zhukov unconditionally on May, 2nd, 1945.

On May, 8th German forces surrendered to the Allies and the war in Europe was over.

A giant army was formed by Russian general Rokossovsky, the 1ˢᵗ Belorussian front with a total of one million soldiers.

Later in November 1944 this front was divided and the troops selected to go to Berlin were transferred to General Zhukov.

As this giant army marched to Berlin they were ambushed and severely hit by the Germans. But they continued to march and carried out the offensive called Vistula-Oder and the battle of Halbe and Halter, sixty kilometers from Berlin.

It was January/February 1945.

The Red Army encircled Berlin after the battle of Seelow Heights and on April, 20ᵗʰ; General Zhukov gave the order to shell without interruption Berlin´s center. The other part of this military movement the 2ⁿᵈ Belorussian front and the 4ᵗʰ Ukrainian front with its commanders Konev and Yeremenko supported by an army of two hundred and eighty thousand men.

They bombed during three days and nights non- stop while their main troops remained at ninety kilometers from downtown Berlin.

On May, 2ⁿᵈ, 1945 Germany surrendered.

It had been nearly six years. We did not know about my mother Szjandla and my brother Elia. For sure they will go to the American Zone. Somehow our feeling was that they would have managed to find a way and means to join Jewish groups migrating to Israel. These operated mainly from the American Zone.

We got together six ex Russian combatants and decided to walk from Berlin to Munich. We were decided to survive and did the right thing apparently.

The distance between Berlin and Munich was 504Km.

6-ARE YOU A COMMUNIST?

The Red Army had prepared the revenge of the revenges.

The mother of all revenges!

To show the world, that the socialist movement was strong, that the Soviet Union was its leader and saved the world; this would be the Socialist revenge. They were getting ready for an international propaganda Campaign in favor of Socialism, Marx-Lenin type with a Russian twist: Dominate your friends and exterminate your foes.

We thought of remaining in the Soviet Union after the war mainly because we were standing on their territories but the anti-Jewish culture and the way how most Jews were treated in the armies we met, made us change directions and reconfirm our initial wish: Let´s go to the United States of America!

As soon as we started meeting American soldiers we asked them to show us photos of their country and they gladly did. Usually photos of the family, the friends, their sweetheart or a pin up girl.

It looked nice, family and clean. People were always eating, drinking and smoking.

Slowly we started to find out how this subject of immigration into the USA worked. After some bureaucracy we got to seat individually in front of somebody from the Immigration Department.

-'Name?

-'Majer Korn Miller.

-'Age?'

-' 26'.

-'Position in the Russian army?: Soldier, infantry.

-'Since when? Since the beginning of the invasion of Poland by the Germans. September, 1939.'

-'Is your family from German Origin?' No

-'But your surnames are Germanic'.

-'Yes, But the family is Jewish'.

-'Do you have family or friends in Russia?'

-'No' I do´t-'

-'But your brothers?

-'No, they are with me'.

-'They also were part of the Red Army?'

-'Yes, we all run away from the German army when the SS invaded our hometown.' Sorry I confused things. Myself and my two older brothers went to Russia; But my younger brother stay with our mother, hidden by the peasants and protected by the partizanim

-'Name of the town you were born?'

-'Tarnogrod'.

-'Was there a Communist Party or club or Socialist association in Tarnogrod?'

-'No, I really don't know. I never heard of this when I lived there.'

-'Address for correspondence?'

-'Sorry?'

-'Where do we send you a letter'.

-'I don't know. Now I am in the Russian army'.

-'I don't think we send letters to them'.

-'Sorry', please wait a few days and I will inform an address to send correspondence.'

-'Sorry, cannot. When you are ready come back.'

-'Yes, Sir, Bye'.

-'Bye'.

Our American's dream was over temporarily!

For the Russians, the stone in the shoe was the American Army equipped with the best, the newest and had apparent limitless resources.

Going back, on April 25th the encirclement finished and soviets and Americans soldiers met at Torgau on the shores of River Elbe.

A few days later run the news that Hitler committed suicide. The gossip that lasted for a few weeks was that Hitler was taken alive by the Russians and that their intelligence unit NKVD was interrogating him about hideouts of art objects and gold bars.

When we were able to move around part of the city we saw the soviet flag raised over the Reichstag, seat of the German Parliament.

But going back in time, a few dramatic years, things were different.

We did our Exodus in September, 1939. We focused firstly in finding a place for my parents and for Elia, my younger brother. Meanwhile we slept at a barn with some animals and did small jobs for food and hot tea.

We survived well and we were being pushed by the local commissar to go to adult school where we would learn about socialism and normal studies. We spent nearly one year being slippery and avoiding this school and funny teachings.

Honestly, most displaced persons as us participated in the school for adults.

My brothers and I were nearly ready to give in when the news came that Germany has invaded Russia. This was in June, 1941.

Plans changed and the commissar preferred to see us in military training for civilians. The Russians organized the men and started training heavily; Physical and fire arms routines in the morning and political indoctrination in the afternoon. Sometimes in the middle of the night while warm.

In the Camps while resting somebody would ask the commissar what happened to the friendship agreement with Germany, why was Russia invaded?

The commissars in charge of political discipline always tried to avoid a direct answer. Again we heard gossip about slave labor Camps mainly for Jews, Gypsies, blacks and political opposition members in Germany.

The answer to the question was given with an ugly face; typical of those who ate something sour and did not like it.

-'At the time the agreement seemed to be the best choice for the soviets'- answered the commissar' – and continued – ' during wartime some rights have to be suspended'.

Would they feed these slaves enough to survive and work hard or less than needed so slowly they would be killed of malnutrition and related diseases?

Initially Germany's invading forces were expecting success as they had a few months before when invaded France and The Netherlands.

Mission "Barbarossa" was Hitler's code name of the invasion plan to occupy the Soviet Union by German Troops and their forces were trained for immediate occupation. That was the standard comment with officers and comrades;

First, the bombing of military targets for three days and nights, nonstop. Then the infantry would occupy a geographical section of land near Leningrad and after having controlled certain area by the troops, special military units of SS and Military Police, would screen in every town or city for unwanted persons, especially male Jews, political activists, candidates for resistance and others.

In a few months the German troops had advanced to the gates of Leningrad, took Smolensk, encircled Dnepropetrovsk in Ukraine and reached the outskirts of Moscow by December 1941.

The Red Army who had taken a beating started to resist and fight back while stopping the German advances.

All this information was given at the political education hour by the commissar and his assistants.

Soon the Germans were exhausted. They didn't expect the invasion and conquest of Russia to take so long. They also made big mistakes in planning and operations of their logistics causing lack of food.

Many losses had the Germans and the Red Army after they decided to counterattack. But the Germans insisted, at a very high human and resources cost, and in the summer of 1942 they were putting pressure on Leningrad.

A Russian counteroffensive occurred in the same year; a German offensive failed in Kursk; in 1943 the Germans were pushed back to the Dnieper River; in July 1944 the Russian troops reached East Prussia and in January 1945 they were in the banks of the Oder. Here they established their bridgehead and launched a massive attack on Berlin.

Berlin fell and Germany surrendered unconditionally on May, 7, 1945 at the east and May, 9th, 1945 at the west.

Victory day was proclaimed on May, 8, 1945. All above information was given in our political instruction classes.

Our only source of information, since radio or newspaper was not available.

Until now I have only written down historical events given in our Russian political class hours. I will write now about me, my feelings, my brothers, my comrades and my new country, although temporarily. I comment this because I plan to travel when the war is over.

At night sometimes a wake up to see if I am really sun bathing on a tropical beach; then I stand up and go outside and it was very cold. Some comrades were doing night watch duty and I could heart their chatting about leaving the Red Army as soon as a peace agreement is reached. It has been said that the powerful war machines of the USSR and USA and their allies would destroy the German infantry same as they did with the navy and air force.

A few days later still had some shooting going on, by independent idiots for sure, reminded everybody that the war just ended.

On a warm Sunday morning we met some neighbors from Tarnogrod walking from Bielorussia, very religious Jew, married, two children and after we told them we fought the war in the Red Army he asked :

-'Are you communists?

-'No, never! – we answered.

-' Why?' –asked the religious Jew.

-'I respect people and hate slavery'-

-' Your parents were also anti-communists?''

-'Yes; I respectfully understand the Germans were an enemy for the free world and especially for the Jews –'the Russian Jews or Non-Jews.

-'If we did not join the Red Army at the beginning we would surely be dead'- commented my brother .

-' Although we fought for the Red Soviet Army we were not communists. Not even a little bit. We preferred to be alive. We were anti-German!'

One of the Tarnogrod neighbors started to make questions and declarations. Suddenly the one acting as an interviewer started to lecture:

"Jews have a close relationship with Marxism. That is what some smart people said. Some intellectuals pinpointed that Talmudic Judaism is the father of modern Communism. To add something: Karl Marx was from a Jewish family of rabbinical descent. The smart commentators continue saying that Marx filtered Talmudism for Gentile consumption.

Another Jew called Moses Hess of similar origin as Marx thought in the 1870's that Communism could best be achieved on a world wide scale through Jewish Hasidism and Zionism, based upon Orthodox Judaism. Mr. Hess worked and agitated together with Marx and Engels.'

Somebody interrupted:

-'So what that Marx descended from a Jewish family; so did Jesus Christ.'

The man lecturing, stopped and looked over the top of his eyeglasses to the people in the auditorium moved his nose as if smelling something rotten and continued:

-'The Soviet revolution of 1917 involved many intellectuals and people with a high personal discipline and within these many Jews such as Kamenev and Trotsky."

To make it short there is no conflict in being Jewish and communist except that part related to God. Atheist, or not? In theory you could be Jewish and be at the extreme and not believe in God!

I had mixed feelings about the mental sanity of my interviewer but he behaved like a professor and said things convinced that they were true.

-'Lenin was he a supporter of Jewish emancipation?'- I asked- '- would he had us transported to Siberia?'.

-'Unfortunately, comrade Lenin thought different' – he said and continued - 'I will repeat if my memory allows me a sentence of Lenin with regards to policy in Ukraine:

"Jews and city dwellers of the Ukraine must be taken by hedgehog-skin gauntlets, sent to fight in front lines and should never be allowed on any administrative positions (except a negligible percentage, in exceptional cases, and under our class control)".

So, very pragmatically Lenin was recreating an intellectual Ghetto for Jews in the Ukraine. Stalin declared once that Bolshevism had two factions: 'The Jewish faction' and 'the true Russian faction'.

At the end of the war (1944-1945) and for a few years, anti-Jewish violence in Poland was publicly known and probably remained in the unconscious of the surviving Jewish people.

There were individual attacks and organized collective attacks.

Programs, as they were called, were the result of these attacks whose characteristics were basically to eliminate the Jews by insulting, lying about their culture, destroying their property and hurting them physically.

The psychological source of the event, the inner component, was the preaching against Jews. This was the "warm up".

The immediate result of this violence was the Jewish emigration from Poland: Jews that survived the WW2 in Poland and those returning from the Soviet Union. It can be said that the return of so many

Jews, after the war, from Russia created a local resentment towards the returning people mainly because they would reclaim their properties who had already been taken by poles.

They were counted in tens of thousands. Before the WW2 it was possible to count them in millions.

Blood libel rumors caused most Programs against Jews and a minor cause was that the introduction of Stalinist communism was the responsibility of Jews since many occupied high positions in the new government controlled by Russia and the Communist Party.

A typical blood libel against Jews was the Jews kidnapped gentile children for ritualistic activities, mass murder of non-Jewish children.

A group of anti-Jewish people would get together in a plaza, or coffee house or bar and start spreading lies about a child kidnapping on a Saturday during Jewish Sabbath prayers; or about a Saturday blood drinking session.

After getting the crowd excited and drooling they would walk to the nearest synagogue and start insulting the Jews that were in it, then pushing some of them, throwing stones and beating some of them with pieces of wood. Some were left with broken noses, broken arms and torn clothes. Some were robbed by the mob. Some had their shops and offices destroyed and burnt

Suddenly the news of kidnapping and blood ritual, supposedly practiced by Jews, would spread out and many towns would start their own Program against the local Jews.

For these events and also because Poland allowed Jews to migrate to Palestine, many Jews started their own "Exodus" and left Poland after the war. The death toll for the Jewish population in Poland due to anti-Jewish activities conducted by Polish people at the end of the war and mostly just after the WW2 is to be counted in thousands of innocent people dying for hate reasons.

Another myth introduced by the anti-Jewish Polish forces was the "Zydokomuna" (judeo-communist) myth that considered there was a Soviet-Jewish collaboration to import Stalin's communism into Poland.

Holding Jews responsible for the forced introduction of communism, into Poland's life.

Two main facts turned this myth into a believer's wishful truth: the fact was that thousands of Jews were returning after the war from the Soviet Union.

And that within the high politically powered people, there were many of Jewish background holding jobs in the Polish United Workers Party, Ministry of Public Security, and State Security Services.

After the war, and also for internal security reasons, it was very difficult for a single guy, ex-soldier of the Red Army, suspected of being a member or at least a collaborator of the communist ideology, to get a decent job in the USA. Of course first we needed to get an entry visa with a work permit.

During the WW2 the American communist party organized itself to take advantage of the "return home" of the soldiers that spent a few years with the armed forces and now had to decide between studying and working.

Communism was a frightening animal trying to help the Soviet Union become the world's dominator and creating an internal USA response with the imprint of Senator MacCarthy.

This Senator and his followers set themselves to help the USA get rid of communists and other, so called, traitors.

Many liked communism because it represented the forces of anti-Fascism and of freedom. Especially, with the intellectual classes, with the unions and students.

An extraordinary witch hunt started in the USA at all levels. In the middle of this turmoil, to try to obtain an entrance visa was very hard. Even worst, if you were a suspect!

This news arrived via newspapers and comments of the American staff of the Camp and sometimes supervisors working for the army.

Although ideological the dispute between Capitalism and Communism was also pragmatic. People would comment that both won the war against Germany, Italy and Japan. Although against Japan mainly the USA, Australia and the British fought and won.

Both countries were of large population and the USA was many times richer than Russia. Both dealt in similar ways with dissidents of their ideology.

Russia persecuted, jailed and executed those against socialism and those who dared speaking out against Stalin; and the USA, with McCarthism very active also persecuted, jailed and segregated those against capitalism. It seemed that it did not matter what extreme of the disease you were, violence was the means to keep the truth with you.

Apparently a simple idea, equality, caused for centuries a violent discussion:

Are all men equal or not?

If they were different, this difference should be naturally accepted so everyone deserves genetically his future or men were not equal and those better prepared will develop strengths that differentiate them from others?

By better prepared, it is meant genetically acquired and educated via learning or experience.

Anyway, going back, we were asked if we were communists. Nearly an insult when you deal with simple people that just wanted to survive. But we were denied entrance to the USA and therefore we needed another option. The reason for the denial was "unfit for the USA" but the real reason was 'too poor to live in the USA'.

The three of us had nothing and were single. Negative options were Europe, Middle East, and Far East. So basically left to choose was Latin America. Not to be boring, we selected by cost and easy to approve visas.

As a result the only place available was Bolivia. We visited every Consulate in Munich and in 1951 we had been visiting Chile, Argentina, Ecuador and Bolivia. Just before we had (and by this time other 5 families joined us) another depressive evening, we received a positive signal; the Bolivian Vice- Consul informed that the group of families that applied for visa was been considered approved. My brother´s had decided and moved to Israel.

How much do we know about it? How many Jews live there? Who are their neighbors are? Who is the Mufty of Jerusalem?

The answers came rather quickly: we know little about Bolivia; there were nearly one thousand Jewish people and Bolivia's neighboring countries are Paraguay, Peru, Chile Brazil and Argentina.

The cost of each visa (family) was five hundred American dollars and the diplomat in charge was the Vice Consul in Munich.

In 1933 when Hitler gained political power in Germany there were thirty Jewish families in Bolivia and by 1942 were estimated about seven thousand.

During the period of 1938-1940, Maurice Hochschild, a Jewish businessman with investments in Bolivia, helped creating the "Sociedad de Protección a los imigrantes Israelitas" (Protection Society for the Jewish immigrants) and together with the Sociedad Colonizadora (Settler's Society) developed agricultural projects which did not succeed; and slowly Jews migrated from Bolivia to the neighboring countries, such as Argentina and Chile.

7-SWITCHING SIDES

Going back in time.

When we marched in 1945, with the Red Army into Germany, the obsession with changing sides woke up. We needed to abandon the Red Army; we had done our job and did not feel at home with them.

We were given protection against the Nazis and we have paid for it fighting a real war for the Russians and helping win the war.

It was early morning and we were about five hundred meters from the US Army. Many soldiers of the Red Army risked being disciplined by a superior or a party commissar by going near the American troops for cigarettes and chocolate bars both for consumption and for business.

Me and my brothers got up and walked in the direction of an American soldier taking photos. The soldier looked very young and did not seem to be a warrior. We got near him and waved. He waved back.

-'Do you speak Russian?'- He waved his head meaning negative.

-'Do you speak Polish?' - The same negative movements.

-'German?'

He answered - 'a bisale' (a little, in Yiddish). So we found a Jewish American soldier! From now on it will be Yiddish! -'I am Majer' - Introduced myself with my finger pointed to my nose – 'Wolf and Haim' - pointing to my brothers:

-'Yes' – We all answered.

-'So you were Polish Jews in the Red Army? Majer, Wolf and Haim?'- He repeated.

-'Yes' – We all answered again in unison

-'My name is Henry Cohen. American Jew from Brooklyn, New York'- he offered a cigarette which Haim promptly accepted.

We needed to trust him so we did not waste too much time.

-'We are brothers'- I said - 'We want to change sides'.

-'What do you mean by change sides'? – The American asked.

-'We need to abandon the Red Army and go to a refugee Camp in your zone. The American zone' - and continued - 'We are not Russians. Please let us in!, Henry Cohen. We are Polish Jews.'

-'We run away from the Germans in our small town, crossed the border with many others into Russia and were transformed into Russian soldiers that fought its way to Berlin. Now we want to change sides.

Change to your side. Please help!'- was Haim′s appeal.

Sounded more like a prayer, than just a simple appeal.

-'I am not a fighting soldier. I am from the administration group. You should go by yourselves to refugee or displaced person' s meeting points. But let me check with the Major' – and he left us standing while he walked back where some troops were resting and talked to a tall soldier. In a few minutes he was back and said:

-'Ok, we will give you a lift. We are going to Munich and nearby there will be a labor Camp that is being prepared to receive DPs.'

-'Thank you, thank you very much. But what is the meaning of DPs?'

-'DP means Displaced Person' – He said -'there I may be able to help you locate your landsmen.'

In less than one hour we were riding in the back of an American army truck, seating at the open back together with other ten American soldiers. There were many hours and many stops to check at American checkpoint. Somebody mentioned that the trip was especially for Henry Cohen. He was going to be a Senior Administrator of some sort in the DP system being installed. Each zone had their refugee's Camp and the Americans had and managed the largest.

They needed to deliver him at an US Army center near Munich. That is why we were driving there. Finally a large city appeared. It was called Nuremberg and it looked nearly destroyed by the bombing; they told us there was a few months ago a fierce five day battle between Germans and USA forces. The city looked devastated.

We passed thru very quickly and stopped at the American quarters about one hour later. Had some warm canned food, a small rest and continued travelling.

Regensburg seemed from the truck, to have suffered little damage; and later passed thru Augsburg whose center we drove thru and it was totally destroyed. The soldiers with us say the target of the British RAF and USAIR Force was the works of Messerschmitt, the German's war plane manufacturer.

It must have been a very strategic target because tens of blocks of buildings were totally on the ground not leaving one wall standing up. At the time we passed by there were some shadows moving in between the debris picking up things and then throwing them far away.

I asked the sergeant sitting next to us if he spoke German or Polish or Yiddish and he looked in my eyes and said English and a bit of Yiddish.

-'So you are Jewish American. How come?' -'My parents were Polish Jews that migrated to the United States about fifteen years before the war and established themselves in New Jersey next door to New York'. I understand you three are brothers?

-'Yes, we are'.

-'Where are you from?'

- 'From Tarnogrod, Poland'.

-'How did you survive?'

-'We escaped Hitler's SS, spent time hiding in the forests and when the Nazis and Russians started fighting each other, we came out of hiding and joined the Soviet's army. Had a little training as soldiers by the Russians and we were sent to the front. We are lucky to be here!'

-'Yes, you are lucky. Have you seen the concentration Camps?' – asked the American and looked to me and my brothers very serious.

-'No, we have heard but have not seen them.'- answered Wolf.

-'How are they? Is it true that people had forced labor like slaves? That Jews worked until total exhaustion before collapsing and dying? - asked Haim.

The sergeant looked at us very worried of what he was preparing to say, As if he was choosing the right words.

-'It was shocking! I could never have imagined the atrocities these Nazi people committed and in the last few weeks before we reached Munich tried to hide. They murdered Jews by millions; first, forcing them to work, then exterminating them as worms with toxic gases and shooting. Then they cremated their bodies. Men, old people, women and children' – said the American. -'How was it possible?' – I asked- nobody spoke out, nobody heard or saw anything?

- 'We do not know, but we will find out and punish the murderers that survived. This was done with people as simple as a janitor to people as sophisticated as bankers, executives, professors. Everybody knew!' – answered Henry.

-'When did you find out this?' – asked Haim – 'we were here and never heard much of it.

-'As soon as we approached Munich we entered one of such concentration Camps and thru interrogation of prisoners and guards that survived we found out that rumors were true. Most of it was reconfirmed by our Chaplains who spoke more than once with Jews that survived the gas chambers and after been fed and regained part of their forces wanted to talk and share their tragic moments'.

-'Many survivors?' – asked Wolf.

-'No, very few. Some died after our interview but left their witness to history.'

-'Your intelligence services must have estimated how many were sacrificed at the Camps?' – my brother asked.

-' Our intelligence division was ordered to find out how fiercely the Germans would defend themselves and discovered the 'last line of defense that Hitler ordered to defend him and his inner group: they were old men and children; that were our orders we approached Munchen'.

He gave us his hand and mumbled something and left back to their barracks, Near midnight we arrived at the army Camps outside Munich. We drove thru part of the town and it looked very heavily damaged by the Allies Airforce.

Henry Cohen allowed us to sleep in the dormitories and recommended us to wake up early, get a ride into Munich and find the American Army General Affairs office. Once there, ask for refugee or Displaced Persons facilities.

At this office we could find out if people from our Tarnogrod had appeared in Germany in the American Zone. If a DP person appeared to US military they would direction him to General Affairs Office who was making the lists by names, city and country of origin, birth date, name of father and mother. These

52

edited lists were then printed and distributed within the General Affairs offices of the US military in Germany.

In about two hours, by army truck, we got to this office in Old downtown Munich, the famous Altstadt near the Opera House.

We were given books with the names of Polish Jews from Lublin's province, including the town of Tarnogrod people, that were at this displaced persons Camp about thirty kilometers from there on the highway to Garmish Partenkirchen. The only way to get there was thru army transport, either jeep or truck.

After a few hours search thru the names, Wolf found a familiar name: Kamerman, Oskar and another school friend of mine, Bluma Haller now Kamerman. There were other Hallers but none of us had met them before.

A connection with Tarnogrod found after nearly six years! Few Jews born in Tarnogrod survived. The main reason was that more than fifty percent of the Jewish families were very religious and refused to run away when the Germans were coming. Some because they waited for the Messiah and would not fight back; also because it was Rosh Hashanah when the Nazis came into town and because of the Sabbath.

How did Oskar manage to get to Germany so fast?

To get our younger brother Elia and our mother in Germany was essential to plan immediately.

Next morning after travelling for one hour we were at Wolfratshausen, a small town near an ex- forced labor Camp called Foehrenwald. After asking some peasants, that were walking on the side of the road, how to get there we walked according to their directions.

As we got nearer, from the distance, we could see the large triangular-front type of houses and later presented us at the main entrance. As the three of us arrived, the guards began to scream in English, and ten soldiers came running to the main doors.

We were interviewed in a small warm room by two Americans and forms were filled and signed. They were worried and upset with us. After some screaming from them, I deducted the reason: we were dressed in Russian uniforms and wearing Russian boots and looked like Russians.

Later we were told that one of their worries was that we could be Nazis wearing Russian uniforms and passing by German Jews. It had happened according to their intelligence services and they were very nervous about this possibility.

A Jewish Chaplain, a Reform Rabbi from New York, was called to certify we had Jewish religious upbringing and it was done in a short time. Then we were authorized to go ahead.

When everything was done we managed to get our entry application approved.

As soon as we entered the Camp we were given two double-decker beds, and we went out in search of Tarnogroders.

After some time walking around the periphery of the Camp we found Blima, Roza's sister in a waiting queue for food. She got the food needed and together we searched for Oskar. He was in a political meeting of Betar, a Jewish political party with right wing trends. He was a fighter and did not like the Russians or bolsheviques or Reds or soviets and he had witnessed together with a small group of Partisan massacres committed by the Red Army in occupied Poland.

In the meantime a Jewish Partisan Group with left wing tendencies, and that worked very close to soviet intelligence in Poland, had rescued my mother Szjandla and my younger brother Elia, and they plus others that were together and all were delivered to a refugee group in northern Germany. They knew Oskar from the guerilla war in the woods in Poland and they were being sent as DPs to the same Camp in Foehrenwald.

Blima, Oskar's wife, had gone to School with me and we had a friendly relationship.

They had saved Fayga and my mother and thru partisan's connections flown into Germany. Arrived in Regensburg and trucked till Wolfratschausen and then to the DP Camp in Foehrenwald. The reason for this special treatment to Oskar's group was his knowledge and live witness as partisan, of the Katyn massacre.

This event was a series of massacres occurred in Poland in between April and May, 1940, where nearly twenty two thousand Polish military, government, intellectuals, poets, politicians were murdered by the NKVD (Soviet Secret Service).

The western allied intelligence services wanted him alive. That is why Oskar and family were flown into Germany. Like him many others were protected to be witnesses of history.

Oskar's legs had started to trouble him. The doctor in the American zone had informed him that he suffered from diabetes and because of it, leg pain and cramps occurred as a result of a form of nerve damage. The doctor also said that besides pain, tingling and numbness are also common. All these sensations he felt and he knew he was debilitating. The only solution was to keep blood sugar level controlled.

'Take care' - said the American doctor – 'we need you alive and well'.

A few days later two of Oskar's colleagues in the Partisan group were seen at the Foehrenwald Camp talking to a Senior Administration executive, an American.

They invited the two Partisans to enter and sat down in an office without windows and placed two guards at the single entrance door; they came to talk to me since they knew me and Oskar were acquainted.

I informed Oskar was in a Betar meeting and would last another two hours. It was surprising the positive energy from people so that life returns to normal as soon as possible. So Jewish political life was having its rebirth and business was hectic, commerce growing and black market too.

The Americans asked me to say that Oskar was presumed dead and his wife too. Apparently friendly fire, from the Polish Army. The official version was that he had been picked up in Poland by a US Force Cargo plane together with his family and that a few seconds after takeoff, somebody (presumably Polish Army Intelligence) had shot the plane and it exploded in the air, burning and destroying all equipment, passengers and crew.

I repeated exactly what I was told. The two visitors did not seem to be satisfied. After they said goodbye they asked for formal permission to visit the site of the accident. The Americans promised to send the coordinates needed to locate the exact spot. The two visitors were Poles probably under NKVD orders to try to eliminate all witnesses of the Katyn events. Even those who shot the Polish intelligentsia and prominent people.

I suppose they never did. Oskar, his wife Bluma and their two girls went to live in Sydney, NSW, and Australia.

8-THE CAMP

Camp Foehrenwald was one of the largest displaced persons (DPs) centers in Germany. It was located about twenty three kilometers south of Munich, Foehrenwald, Wolfratshausen. DPs meant really refugees

It worked around a village built in 1939 for up to three thousand people for the I.G.Farben Group to house its slave workers for munitions plant, well camouflaged by the forest. The conglomerate called I.G. Farben was the largest German group of the Nazi era.

Just before surrender in 1945 they controlled two hundred and forty four companies some of them already important by themselves: BASF, BAYER, AGFA, HOECHST and others.

Camp Foehrenwald, during WW2, was a forced labor manufacturing unity, sub Camp of Dachau Concentration Camp.

Many DP (Displaced Persons) were transferred from other Camps such as Feldafing and Landsberg in late 1945, when Eisenhower, Commander-in-Chief of the Allied Forces, visited crowded Feldafing Camp and touched with what he saw and heard, he ordered afterwards, Foehrenwald to become exclusively a Jewish Camp.

In 1946 an UNRRA,(United Nations Relief and Rehabilitation Administration) team took over the management of the Camp.

By then already five thousand six hundred inhabitants lived in the Foehrenwald Camp in housings with over twenty five people. Beds were double-decker, two persons sleeping in each bunk. The families were separated by blankets hanging from the ceiling.

Six hundred toilets were available at the Camp.

The UNRRA team worked also on rehabilitation, organizing self governance teams, skills development, drama, athletic programs. A group of Jewish displaced persons published a newspaper called Bamidbar in Yiddish.

In parallel about three hundred and fifty youth were organized in Kibbutzim to learn agricultural and trade skills. These Zionist communes represented the spectrum of Jewish politics after the war: Kadima, Dror, Bnai Akiva, Poel Ha-Dati, Ohel Sarah, Agudat Israel and various others.

Everything, with the intention to bring back self- esteem and positive thinking to the Displaced Persons.

As life was getting on, bad news started to come in from Poland. Some we initially thought exaggerated but sooner than we could imagine these news were confirmed

Progroms were conducted by Poles unhappy with the situation of a partially destroyed country by the Germans and the Russians, initially and later by the takeover of the Soviet Red Army.

Some poles persecuted Jews and other minorities that survived and, sometimes beat them to death.

These Progroms were result of social frustration and a change in motivation apparently. Since Jews could not be blamed for the results of WW2 other social minorities were blamed inclusive the Americans and British. These last ones took a long time to declare war on Germany. Britain and Poland had a mutual defense agreement.

Special attention was given to Kielce's Progrom on July,4th, 1946 and before that, Lublin's Progrom of November,19,1945.

As a result 43 Jews were killed in cold blood and in public.

Back in the Camp we were trying to have a normal life by doing normal things and participating in normal events. Although, it may not seem normal to some people.

In this collective spontaneous effort to live a normal life, or life as usual, Camp Foehrenwald became the center of Chassidic life in the American protected zone. Important Rabbis came to visit the Camp and made donations.

A Jewish police force and a fire brigade were organized by the Camp's management. There was a gossip between some Jews that the Jewish Youth of the Camp were being trained by members of the embryonic cells of the Jewish Army to be (Haganah).

The war ended in May, 1945, and the Nazis were defeated and their country nearly destroyed. Still, anti-Judaism continued to exist.

Its clearest manifestation was in the tense relationship that occurred from time to time with the American soldiers who brought within themselves, home grown feelings about Jews.

Relations with locals with regards to black market and with the defeated Germans that were neighbors of the Camp, or had to work and cohabitate with the Jewish Displaced Persons or with the American victors.

These Displaced Persons, infiltrated into Germany in large numbers because of the existing feeling of safety in the American zone.

Fewer people wanted the Russian zone because of historical confrontational events between their countries and the Russian Empire and later on, with the Soviet Union. Some chose the Soviet's side for purely ideological reasons. Racism was also a social disease within the Russian armed forces and from there to Anti-Judaism it was just a small road. Again a good example on how to use Racism for unification causes confusing nationalism or patriotism with it.

The Camp became well known, in the Jewish world, and many important and distinguished personalities visited it while it operated as a DP Camp; just to name a few top brass of the American military and the Rabbi Chaim Herzog, Chief Rabbi of Palestine; as an example of distinguished visitors.

After one year in the Camp, my brothers Wolf and Haim already had their business making clothes for men and women. All type of dresses from a simple daytime party wedding to a nearly black tie.

They wanted to save US Dollars for their trip to Israel, for their 'real' wedding and to pay for an upgrade after they had a child. A living quarter's upgrade. Both Haim and Wolf got married before the end of the war, just by word compromise; they wrote to their future wives who lived in Russian controlled towns with their relatives.

After the end of WW2 they called their wives to Foehrenwald and got married with a Rabbi and official registration. They worked very hard and the Camp was growing with people, noisy, smelling food and after two years, by the end of 1947, they had packed some reselling goods and saved enough dollars to travel to Israel, which they did.

Wolf, wife and two children left first. A month later left Haim, his wife and one boy. They planned to have their business in Tel Aviv.

I thought, but I had to check with my wife, to follow them but first would like to put together more reselling goods and dollars.

Three years later, I was ready to leave Europe but not to Israel. I had two partners in a silverware shop and slowly was making enough to pay the bills and retain some dollars.

In 1946 appeared Elia and my mother. He had grown up and my mother Szjandla was "sick from the nerves". It meant, early "dementia" a progressive disease. They came to live with us.

After nearly two months my brother Elia started to talk funny and stutter.

I remember saying: '-Calm down Elia. What is it? - Roza's friend will find a nice Jewish girl from a nice and important Jewish family for you at the Camp'.

-'Thanks, but it is not that, I want to migrate to Israel' – said Elia.

My mother decided to speak: -'I am the oldest of the family here and can decide: if you marry you can go!'.

He found a pretty girl, married her in 1946 and by 1951 they already had two children, he had packed and was ready to go to Israel thru a Zionist organization taking Jewish families in needy conditions, to live there.

Myself married Roza, in January 1948, my school friend Bluma's sister who lived with her at the Camp. For some time we dated and went out as sweethearts with Roza and Fayga as super-chaperon. Rozas`sisters insisted on this scheme although none of us was from a traditional family; not traditional in the sense of conservative and against changes, especially modernizations.

I had been ready to pack and go too. But in a conversation with my wife I was surprised by her firm position. She said she was strongly against going to participate in another war or even be near of any war for any reason. That she knew of details of the war between the Arabs and the Jews. She and her son would not go to Israel or any part of Europe.

I could go alone with my mother.

-'But my three brothers are there. They are establishing themselves and could help us'- I said to my wife.

-'I and any child we may have in the future will not go!'- She confirmed without hesitation –' I wasn´t born to be in wars; I did not spent this war kneeling in a hole to choose war again!' - And slowly started to cry.

-'And myself where will I stay?

In an old people´s home?'- said my mother.

-'No Bube, you can stay with us' – Answered my wife -'wherever we go you come together'.

'-But Roza I have already sent a truckload of silverware to Israel. What to do?'- I complained again.

-'Ask your brothers to sell it and send you the money or resend the silverware back here'- answered Roza.

-'Let´s solve one problem at the time'. My brothers are in Israel and life there is complicated'- made a pause and continued - 'so again, my mother stays or goes always with us? '.

-'Fine'- said mother -'and where are we going? Not Europe'- she finished with a deep breath filling her lungs with air. Proud of her achievement to make me change my plans and deeply satisfied that future meant together with her family, or at least partially together.

By the end of 1949 Roza was expecting a child and judging by the size of her belly, was enormous,

The child was born in October, 1949. The weather was chilly for days.

He was a baby boy and everybody thought he was calm and soft tempered. The type of baby that let everyone sleep at night.

On the eight day of his birth, the ritual Jewish circumcision performed by an old Mohel; neighbors and family members warmed up drinking Vodka, and a few, tea. My wife restarted her pressure Campaign to leave Europe and many times a week asked how things were going with our visas, when expected to travel, when should she start preparing things.

In the meantime business in Munich was improving but the will to leave Europe prevailed.

I did not have answers but many excuses.

There was a large Mizrahi Group; followers of religious Zionism a nationalistic political movement for the establishment of a Jewish homeland. In this group, Jews trace their roots to Muslim majority countries. Normally speaking two or three or more languages: Arabic, French, Spanish and Ladino. Many learnt Yiddish but kept Sephardic traditions. Their Leader a Rabi sent his nephew to talk with me.

He came in the shop, introduced himself and gave as address the Foerhenwald Camp.

-'So we are neighbors in Foerhenwald' – I said.

-'Yes, thank god for a peaceful place' – answered the new neighbor.

-'What can I do for you? Would you like to see some object?' – I offered.

-'I do not understand about silver but the menorah looks very pretty'- he commented.

-'My name is Majer Korn, born in Poland'-presented himself my father.

-Nice to meet you. My name is Daniel Gattelli – said my new neighbor, born in Cairo, Egypt.

My father decided to invite him for a hot drink to a coffee shop one block away and Daniel accepted. While walking Daniel inquired if the silver ware shop was for sale. '-I heard you are leaving Europe soon and you are selling the commercial point and stock'- Daniel said

-'Yes, eventually we will sell when we decide where to go' -answered my father.

-'Do you have interest'? – asked my father

-'My family has been in your shop, everybody likes it and think your sales methods to be very modern' – replied the neighbor.

-'Thank you Majer for the reception'- complimented.

-'Listen Daniel the shop will close in 30 minutes. We can take the train together to go to the Camp'; and if you wish you can participate in a Camp Board Meeting. I am a member' – finished Majer.

During the trip my father explained that the Board was under pressure to works inside the Camp and explained while we walked from the station into the Camp.

It seemed difficult to find space for a synagogue, ritual baths and other facilities. With time a Jewish Religious School was available, New Hospital, a Mikveh, a few synagogues were built. Hebrew and Yiddish were taught to the children and technical courses were given for men and woman.

Very quickly its population increased to four thousand DPs where more than five hundred were children under six years old.

All Jewish and therefore very noisy public spaces.

It had its own police and fire brigade; its educational system included some secular schools and the largest Yeshivah in the American's Zone.

There were some professionalizing schools, such as, driver training, beautician and course for nurses. The nurse's course was conducted at the Camp's Hospital; there was also a tailor's school.

Let's open a pause and have back some memories of my son.

The scene I remembered was that he and his friends Adolfo and Norma, whose parents were close friends with mine, walking and running in a field with long grass where he barely was able to keep his head over the grass. They would throw a ball and he would try to catch it.

The children would run and laugh and play until exhausted, then fall on the grass and relax watching the sky.

Most of the time they would hold hands. My son was less than two years old and thought of them as his older brother and sister. This was their daily activity when the weather allowed it. If it was raining they would stay inside the cabin which we shared with two other families.

Every day they played 'hide and seek'. Sometimes, just the three of them other times with two or three neighbors that had their ages.

On the other hand, the adults lived a world of contrasts and paradoxes.

I also remember a speech to a group of neighbors and friends in the Camp that showed my anxiety.

-'I heard that in a military officers meeting they had assumed that most Displaced Persons would be sent to their countries of origin'- said somebody.

-'That is not possible. How can a Polish anti-communist go back to Poland under the claws of the Red Army?'- answered a small voice in the back.

-'They say that the remaining DPs are about one million and basically all refuse to return to their countries of origin'. Jews do not want to go back to the countries were their families had been exterminated and there was local collaboration with the Germans during the war' – said another American officer.

–'Others are afraid to live under a communist regime'- went back one neighbor - and note that in some countries the DP will be considered traitors because in many cases had been Nazi sympathizers' – said the American.

The surviving Jews "non-repatriable", were nearly one hundred thousand.

Totally exhausted and psychologically hurt, people who just survived the war hiding or caged in concentration Camps, were causing major problems to the American military. Most of them were born in Poland.

The idea of sending them back to Poland was being rejected due to information that extra-officially arrived from Warsaw.

In 1946; the Russians repatriated about one hundred a seventy five thousand Jews that fled Poland when the Germans walked in.

But many of these "repatriated" Jews, found some of the Polish people had increased their antiJudaism; so if returned to Poland and stayed, they could not have rebuilt their lives; probably left the country again in search of opportunities in Germany's American Zone.

-'Another problem was the surviving German Jews. They were confusedly considered former enemies by most of the Americans. We need to try harder and help them integrate'- was heard in the Camp.

'It is necessary. But it is so difficult to try and help them'. The challenge was to rebuild their identities on German soil'- said another.

In the Camp there were various organizations trying to help: UNRRA, JDC, JRU, ORT, OSE and the Palestinian Jewish Brigade whose insignia was a yellow David star. These 'Palestinian soldiers' were Jewish and became a symbol within the Camp of Jewish pride, dignity and self-assurance.

By providing a positive view of Zionism, they reinforced the movement for immigration to Israel. As a sort of opposition was the Bund movement, a Jewish socialist movement that believed life existed without Zionism.

Still, Zionists had advantage because most Jews had in their minds that there was one thing they were sure about, that after so many years of persecution, there was no future for Jews in Europe.

Israel was the Jewish Homeland.

Being so the DPs assistance had to be in the sense of giving back their will to live and rebuild their lives. But the horizon was full of problems. One of them was lack of entry visas for the USA, favorite destination for most DPs.

We were witnesses, because present in the Camp from 1945 till 1951, of the efforts of the organizations within Foehrenwald, of the combat of demoralization basically assumed by the military chaplains and under the allied military forces.

The material for the chaplains to work with was of great variety; from rigorous orthodox to fully assimilated, from giving advice; from officiating weddings, preventing the looting of Jewish property, rebuilding cemeteries, establishing school and summer Camps for children, organize list of survivors and help reunite families.

The most incredible of Jewish rebuilding was the authorization to establish training farms backed by UNRRA and financed by JDC.

And these collective farms, called Kibbutzim, a Jewish youth movement guided by a leftist party called "Hashomer Hatzair". These Kibbutzim obtained separate quarters and were highly regarded by the DPs since they fought self destroying inactivity and prolonged internment's psychological negative effects. It was also able to train Jews so they would be prepared to eventually settle and be productive in Israel.

The prototype farm was Kibbutz Buchenwald, at thirty kilometers from Buchenwald, in 1945 produced wheat, sheep, goats and horses. They learnt and practiced the Hebrew language which has also symbolic values such as a shared language to bridge distances between Jews of different nationalities, political and religious affiliations.

The Zionist idea started to make a lot of sense since the survivors had reinforced the idea of a Jewish homeland and this homeland to be called again Israel. But there were also problems with immigrating to Israel because of quotas enforced by the colonial power, Britain.

If to the younger people, Zionism was an ideal, to many older Jews this decision came from a lack of choice and from the desperation to leave life at the Camp.A stronger and new national identity emerged from living in the DP Camps.

The rebuilding of this identity emerged in the Camps caused by the experiences in the WW2 and the difficult living conditions. Establishing families was a building brick in the reconstruction effort especially guided,but not exclusive, for the children thru local Camp school, Hebrew classes, dancing and singing folk music, celebration of religious holidays and preparation for emigration.

A stonewall on the way was prepared by the British with various obstacles to migrate to Israel.

But an opening occurred thru the preparation and later readiness of nearly three thousand young people being done in Kibbutzim in Germany and Austria and later sent to the Middle East as a cohesive group, well educated and well trained and with a vision of mother country and future for their children.

'Mandate Palestine' for the British, was going to become the Land of Israel. After a few years, Wolf, Haim and their families were able to migrate to the USA and establish themselves near New York. They worked until their final years in the clothing industry.

9 – THE NANNY

I tell this story as if I was viewing it today. Chronologically impossible since it occurred while I was still in my mother's belly and in the sequence, just born. This story came in pieces from various sources and it was corroborated by my father and a neighbor. It appeared to me as a basic concept and later started growing with additional information in layers of short stories and details

The week before I was born in Foehrenwald, in the DPs Camp, a delivery truck of small size arrived at the door of the house where my parents and Grandma lived. The driver had to get authorization to enter the Camp, his name and photo were checked twice. Why one could think? The immediate reason: security!

But who would like to enter and rob a Displaced Persons Camp? Well I believe an organization called the miserable people org, is dedicated to that. Something is lost,that is robbed) in the Campo weekly. But that's another story.

When my mother was "very pregnant" walking slightly bent backward pushing the belly forward and complaining to herself of this uncomfortable position.

Being in the extra sensitive situation of being pregnant, she heard someone arrive at the front door, pushed slightly the white curtain and looked out. Now that she was sure that the truck parked at her address she went out to attend this visitor and called my grandma to come out too. Grandma came with a body language saying 'beware rough bodyguard'.

The driver of the truck was a small chubby blonde man doing everything single handed; driving, invoicing and delivering.

He came near the door and knocked on it twice. My mother Roza and my grandma standing together opened the door. Grandma had brought the broomstick with her and left it behind the door. Somebody had told her that unwelcomed visitors leave faster when the broomstick stands behind the door.

My mother with her prominent belly and my grandma wearing a colored cloth on her head. The driver looked at them and smiled.

-'Good morning, ladies'- he said.

-'Good morning'- both answered.

-'Is this cabin 73, Foehrenwald?'

-'Yes'- Both answered.

-'I have a baby carriage to deliver' - and gave my mother three copies of the invoice.

-'One for you, one for the shop and one for me. Please sign you have received and write the date' – he said.

-'Mr. driver, you are making a mistake, this is not mine'- my mother said.

-'Lady, your name is Roza Korn! Yes.

Your address is this? Yes! You expect a baby soon? Yes!

Considering that all your answers were positive then the carriage is yours! Look here, the buyer is Mr. Majer Korn. Do you know him!' – smiled defiantly the driver.

-'He is my husband, but I think he has had some brain lights-out'- and tried to convince the driver that the package was not hers.

-'Please Lady, I have to work and deliver other goods'- and left the package in front of the door while Roza and Bube looked each other not believing what they just heard. After a few seconds both carried it in and left it untouched on the floor.

My father arrived smiling and feeling satisfied, kissed my Grandma and my mother and asked,

-'What´s news?'

-'How can you buy an expensive toy like this? It must have cost a fortune' - answered my mother.

-'Come on let us open the package'– said my father.

The three worked together unpacking the baby carriage. Instructions were written in English and German.

It said "good for babies until three years old". Had four large wheels, blue and white, enough space at the back to carry all necessary things, shining steel and a sun cover.

-'How did you pay for this?' – asked my mother.

-'Yes, how did you pay for this ?' – repeated my grandma smiling defiantly.

-'I sold various pieces of the silver I had in stock, artifacts with a good price and in US Dollars. It was an American officer going back home'- my father said and continued- 'I paid the silver ware to the supplier, paid the rental commission to the shop-owner that lets me use part of his shop as my exhibition room and with what was left I bought the carriage and some food for us. I also bought a new cloth for grandma and wool socks for you both and something special for my wife, a watch' – said my father.

-'So you did a good business deal today'- said my mother.

-'This color I do not use' - said grandma placing it on her head – 'not fashionable'.

It took some time, until dinner was ready, to put together the parts and assemble the baby carriage. It was tall when assembled completely and grandma said she liked it. –'But where did you get the money?'- She continued with her inquiry.

Later in the night my mother sat next to my father in the sofa and asked again:

-'Maybe we could have used this money for other things we need instead of buying a baby carriage for the baby? What did you have in your head?'

-'I saw the carriage in a shop in downtown and I thought: It looks like my son`s car. Went in and bought it for him!' – explained my father.

-'But how about the money?' –asked mother.

-'It was like I told you before. I was at the shop early this morning when an American officer entered and wanted to know how much for a complete silver tableware with 96 pieces and I gave him my full price then he said and how much for those two candelabra and I gave again my full price. Then he thought a little and asked what discount he would get for everything: tableware and candelabra.' – Said father and continued - 'I thought a little, wrote some numbers and answered seven percent discount. He looked at me and gave me a counteroffer: 10 percent discount and he took it all; paid now and sent a truck company to pick it up for him.

I said it is a deal, shook hands and wrote the invoice for which he paid in cash. The rest of the story you know: I went shopping' – father finished satisfied.

Late at night the baby was born at the Foerhenwald Hospital. It was a boy.

A couple of days later was planned to be prepared in the synagogue saloon, on the 8th day after his birth, a simple reception for the ceremony of Brit Milah (Bris) during the morning service. It was the 26th day of October, 1949.

After somebody having verified that there were at least ten Jewish adults the ceremony started with the previous approval and blessing of Grandma. She was looking from the women separate area and trying to keep control on everybody she knew.

The baby was brought into the room where the ceremony would take place by his godmother, who handed him to the godfather, who in turn passed him to the man that held the baby and separated his legs, the Sandek, that put the baby on his knees during the ritual.

The Sandek was a religious man learned in the Torah.

The Mohel performed the ritual and started by instructing the Sandek to hold firm and separated the child´s legs. The Mohel recited a blessing and started the procedure: The father of the baby (that baby was me) recited also a blessing.

The Mohel then removed the baby´s foreskin with a special knife.

Once done, the Mohel drank from a cup of wine and gave the baby his Jewish name.

Following, the Mohel put a drop of wine in the baby´s mouth and the father drank part of the cup and sent the rest of the wine to the mother.

Traditionally the mother waited in a different room where she would receive back the child.

Afterwards there was small reception where grace was recited and a blessing for all main participants was offered: the baby, the parents, the godmother, the godfather and the Sandek. As it was already cold, Vodka was also served early in the morning during the reception.

Somebody managed to bring in a few bottles of Russian Vodka.

Next day, Monday, we were sleeping like in a holiday when the banging of the front door started. My father, simulated being asleep. Grandmother was snoring noisily in the next room, so mother Roza decided to get up and checked who was making noise at this early hour. It was six o`clock in the morning and there was a chubby blond women, early forties, dressed in blue and white, looked like a nurse, smiled and had a happy face.

-'My name is Helga' – she said in perfect German and continued - 'I have come to take care of the new baby'- she finished.

My mother remained wordless and left her standing at the front door.

-'I do not want anyone taking care of the baby except myself'- said my mother thinking of something fishy going on.

-'My name is Helga and I was employed by a manpower Agency for three months. Here look at this service order' – said Helga opening her bag and picking out a piece of paper.

Many things were written on the paper but in her mood, Roza only saw Majer's name signed at the bottom. As she started to turn around Majer appeared in his blue bathrobe and smiled.

-'My name is Majer, please come in'. This is my wife Roza; Grandma and the baby are still sleeping' – father said and indicated to Helga to enter.

'This small confusion was my fault. I decided to give a surprise to my wife so nobody except me and the service agency, knew about the baby having a Nanny for his first three months' – said father.

Nanny Helga blushed and my mother was green with anger.

-'I will explain it to my wife. Fraulein Helga, please take a seat'

Majer took Roza by the hand and both walked holding hands in the direction of the bedroom, closed the door and explained. –'It was supposed to be a nice surprise; a Nanny employed for three months to help with the baby' – said my father apologetically.

-'But I don`t need a German Nanny'! – said my mother.

-'Forget about being German. It was the only Nanny with experience I could find in the agency and I wanted to surprise you and contribute so you would have less work for a few months' – said father.

-'But she will speak in German to the Baby!'- said my mother.

-'You can speak German, Polish and Yiddish, and the baby is too small to make a difference what language he is spoken to' - Majer answered.

-'Also please consider that long before the baby starts to learn to speak, the Nanny will be gone' – Father said.

-'Wait until grandma wakes up and sees a Blonde German Nanny!'- Smiled mother imagining Grandma complaining and mumbling.

-'Wait and see what grandma says about a German blonde taking care of her grandson!' – kept challenging my mother.

Helga did not know what was happening except the surprise. She could not understand our discussion since they were talking mainly in Polish.

She sat silently looking around the cabin and up and down the walls. She was not used to work for non-Germans. Even less so for Jews. But this family seemed to be different. They lived in a displaced persons Camp, in a simple cabin and they had enough money to pay for a Nanny?.

They are prepared to employ a German although they are Jewish. I need the money because in Munich and nearby towns there are no jobs available. I need this job. For three months we can eat at home. -'Maybe' - Helga thought- 'they like me and I can work another few months or find another client here in the Camp'.

After some complaining, like why wasn't she previously consulted, why she always had surprises; Roza accepted the good intentions of my father Majer but was uncomfortable with Helga. She showed the Nanny the new carriage and all together immediately started to re-assemble it. It seemed ready and it was decided to test it before putting the baby in it. 3 of the wheels did not turn easily.

Helga looked, took her jacket off and requested permission to pick up the carriage.

It took her less than thirty minutes and the carriage was re-assembled and ready to go. They took it out for a test drive without the baby. The wheels turned easily! No noise, perfect curves and very light to push.

My mother and Helga, with the empty carriage, went around the block just to see how the carriage managed. A little direction by Helga, a little direction by my mother and both looked at each other and started to smile. Grandma was definitively satisfied with the carriage and a small spark of friendship could be felt in the air.

When they arrived back home, Majer and the baby were awake.

The baby screamed with hunger and for being uncomfortably laid on his pooh. Grandma complained that the baby did not let her sleep.

While mumbling, the door opened and a blond woman pushed a white and blue carriage walked in the front door speaking German to somebody and Grandma caught by surprise thought:

-'Oh my god! The Germans again?'.

Then she repeated it loudly in Yiddish twice.

My mother was just behind Helga and pushed her way in front of her, looked my grandma straight in the eyes and seriously said:

-'Your son decided to give me a surprise and employed Helga, the Nanny, for three months. Her name is Helga and speaks only in German. Please help her and speak to her in German whenever you need whatever you want. Even better, speak to her in Yiddish slowly!' – Mother said.

With a suspicious look Grandma asked:

- 'Where is she going to sleep? Where is she going to eat? What is she going to eat? When?'

My father walked in and said:

-' She will sleep at her home. Comes early in the morning, takes care of the baby and leaves at 4p.m. She will eat with us or wherever she wants. She eats what we eat together with us or alone if she wishes. She stops work for tea twice in the morning and twice in the afternoon. She doesn't work Saturdays or Sundays' – said father.

-'But we eat kosher' – said Grandma.

-'Then she will eat kosher if she wants. If she decides to eat non-kosher it has to be outside' and bring it and get rid of it herself'- answered father and continued- ' kosher food is not so bad and I think she may not even find any difference except, in my opinion, a bit tasteless'.

A big scream followed by smaller ones and finally some sobbing came from the room next door.

Helga immediately asked:

-'Can I go and see him, please?'

-'Yes'- answered Roza.

Suddenly everybody was next to the baby´s bed and my mother picked me up and handed me to Helga. The baby was very wet and she took him to the changing table and asked for some warm water and drying cloth special for babies.

Fraulein Helga showed my mother how to change nappies and wash the baby thoroughly until complete change. The baby was happy and started to make sucking movements with his lips which meant breast feeding.

My mother sat in a large chair, placed a small pillow at her back and received the baby. The baby sucked until he felt asleep. Before, immediately after he finished sucking, he was mumbling and making noises and it appeared to be talking or thanking the breasts for a nice meal.

Very quickly he went into a deep sleep and a few minutes later placed in his bed sideways. Then the women in the house decided to have tea. My grandma, my mother and Helga sat in the kitchen while the kettle was being heated.

My mother served tea to all and asked Helga if she was from Munich. Helga answered yes and before more questions came she started telling her story. She was born in Wolfratshausen and when she was five years old her family moved to Munich due to her father´s working conditions.

There she went to school and then to Teachers Technical School where she learnt to deal with children. Then she met at the Teacher´s School Hans, who a few years later became her husband.

During the war Hans, Herta´s husband was picked up by the SS in a street blitz and placed under arrest. Four weeks went by and Hans still remained under arrest but finally the GESTAPO discovered that somebody had denounced him as having Jewish blood. This event occurred in 1940 and the personal information was kept with its file open until the right opportunity came.

His grandmother was Jewish and his father an assimilated Jew who fought for the motherland in WW1 and was awarded a medal for bravery.

Still the Nazis where after Jews or people with some Jewish blood and although a person who did not practice any religion, he was considered Jewish and sent to Dachau or other extermination Camps.

He was then transferred to forced labor in Foehrenwald I.G.Farben facility until he broke a leg. As it was troublesome to take care of him he was transported back to Dachau where he was exterminated.

-'So he was here at this Camp'- asked my mother.

-'Yes, as far as we know he spent about two months at Dachau before coming to work in the Foehrenwald facility, stayed about six months working and then died in Dachau'- she finished before starting to cry.'

-'I am sorry' – Helga said and cried softly while placing her white handkerchief on her lips.

-'We all suffered during the war and after' - said my Roza – 'but we survived even if some lost parents, brothers and friends'.

-'What hurts me most is that I don´t know for sure where he is buried'-said Helga. 'He was called to serve as police but suddenly he was dropped'. Somebody that knew his family denounced him.

That evening while drinking tea Roza apologized for being so negative at the beginning with Helga, the Nanny. She confessed she was happy inside for the carriage and for having Helga to help. She got closer to Majer and whispered: 'We are all learning to survive'.

Many years later Majer remembered one of the few occasions where my mother recognized he was right were these two events although with some restrictions to be discussed in another day.

Next day Helga arrived early; knocked the door twice. Grandma opened. - 'Good morning Madam'- she said.

-'Good morning, who are you?'- answered grandma to a surprised Helga.

Immediately behind Grandma was standing my mother:

-'Szjandla! Let Helga in. She is the Nanny that was here yesterday'-

-'OK, yesterday we met so many people that I did not remember her face' – said grandma moving aside and letting her inside.

Helga embraced my mother and looked surprised.

Later, when the baby´s nappies were changed, and grandma sat at her favorite chair in the kitchen, and started to sleep with the back of her head against the wall; my mother whispered in Helga`s ear that my grandma was sick.

Her sickness probably caused by what she went thru during the war made her forget most people except my father.

-' So we need to be careful and avoid her picking up the baby, or changing him or cooking with fire or letting her go out by herself'.

And looking tired she continued,

-'In summary, she cannot be trusted to do most things by herself or go out alone'- said mother.

-'I tried to employ somebody for day care for her'- said my mother to Helga but my husband does not believe it is needed.

As she is his mother and he does not see or doesn`t want to see we have been going along as everything is normal. But it is not. Now with the baby we have to be extra careful. Yes?'

-'Yes!'- answered Fraulein Helga.

When Roza cooked, Grandma sat in the kitchen´s stool like a supervisor overseeing somebody else`s work and most of the time slept. When awake she would give her suggestions, such as

-'Put in a carrot and some onions. It gives more taste to the soup'.

-'Medium size potatoes taste better than large ones'.

-'Need a pinch of salt and black pepper'.

-'The gefilte fish needs to be sweet, salty and peppery at the same time'.

-'The horseradish must be sweetish, salty and pepper hot; all at the same time. That is the secret and together with letting it rest for one night before consumption makes a big difference' – said Grandma.

-'Use the bones when making the broth. That is the secret!'- kept on Grandma.

Grandma would repeat above sentences dozens of times per day. After some days Helga got used at not being recognized every morning and sometimes in the afternoon and when at the door she would introduce herself:

-'Helga, the nanny'. Good morning, Madam. Some days, unfortunately only a few people could imagine that life, compared to the war days, was a present from heaven. For some people it was not and they sometime regretted being alive.

Nevertheless they were survivors of a brutal man made catastrophe and to avoid repeating mistakes they had to learn how to survive in a positive way, in a humanistic way; by contributing positively to mankind´s improvement. Everyone knew how to do it and if could not bring it out should keep trying; that just this action is a positive way.

Everyday brought some news about missing people. Some were confirmed dead and some confirmed alive.

They all were just stories to tell but sometimes it felt that to release this pain and share it with others, could somehow damage this painful set of memories. Not damage in the sense of destroying but in exposing something intimate to the public. Each individual knows what was best for himself or herself.

But we need to keep informed the new generations on how we, our parents and grandparents, neighbors and friends survived and participate in the discussions and thoughts about it.

Although nearly five years since the end of WW2 the war was still news.

Helga was well informed about day-to-day business in Germany's political environment. She was explaining that recently, in 1949, from discussions between the four powers, USA, Russia, Britain and France, emerged a new status for Germany.

Instead of one country there were now two countries; West Germany under the guidance of western influence and East Germany under the supervision of the Soviet Union. In August of this year there were elections with the results in favor of Konrad Adenauer whose party was slightly ahead of the second place.

The economy was based on reconstruction of Germany and last year, 1948, Germany was admitted into the advantages of the Marshall Plan that sought to rebuild Europe after WW2.

Also to contain any advances of the Soviet Union's ideology. Where 'Supervision of the Soviet Union' was another phrase for "Communist Control".

Helga, while having a cup of tea, would daily discuss the news with my mother and the presence of Grandma that normally assisted these discussions while sleeping.

My mother's big worry was the possibility of the return of the Nazi party since all big shots available to run the country had some sort of Nazi past, to say the least going up to full membership and behind the curtains participation.

My father would calm her down mentioning the occupation by the allied forces and their complete control of their respective zones.

Also from a pragmatic position, government needed to function and nobody better than old Public Servants to run things smoothly.

The neighbors worried more about the Russians that the improbable return of the Nazis. East Germany was completely under the control and direction of the communist party and this under the guidance of the Soviets. On the other hand West Germany was under control of the USA and her allies Great Britain, France,

This year, after many years of deep misery, Germany shows that prosperity is on its way. TVs become hot stuff. China under the guidance of the Communist Party becomes a communist country and Russia has the Atomic bomb (tested). East Germany chooses its capital: Berlin. West Germany votes Bonn to be its capital.

A big issue is the Berlin blockade. This event started in June, 1948 when the Soviet Union started its blockade of West Berlin so that Germany could not communicate with its capital. Immediately the Berlin airlift started with the Allies intention to deliver food and other important supplies by air. Nearly a year later, in May 1949 the blockade was suspended by the Russians.

Other subjects brought by neighbors and treated as big news were:

RCA America perfected a color TV system, an instantaneous photo camera started to be sold in the USA for US$89,95; brand name Polaroid; the comet airplane built by De Havilland takes its first commercial flight, Apartheid becomes official policy of the National Party of South Africa.

A new tool is announced as the first commercial computer, the Ferranti Mark 1; Frank Sinatra stars with Gene Kelly in "On the Town" and President Truman authorizes US$16 million in aid for Palestinian refugees.

When people got together at the end of the day or on weekends these subjects were the most common to be brought up for discussion, for comments.

Time elapsed and comments within the Jewish community did not change much. The return of people with Nazi background to government jobs was a frightening memory that they could be back.

At the same time some missing war criminals, suspected of having been smuggled out from Germany at the end of the WW2, were seen in places like Argentina, Paraguay, Portugal and others.

It was mentioned that a secret Nazi organization operated transporting, hiding, assisting and giving new identities to Nazi officers and senior government officials.

So Roza insisted in preparing to leave Germany because in her mind when the Allies and the Russians decide to leave Germany it will start all over again and she does not want to be near.

Helga's work satisfied everybody except grandma that each day had to be introduced formally and spent the time she was awake to supervise closely what she was doing and then complain to my mother.

Six months after been born I was well known in the neighborhood. I was a baby that had a German nanny, in a flashy carriage, having every day a stroll around the block in the Foerhenwald DP Camp.

All the neighbors knew the baby by name and when alone they would comment about the blonde nanny.

But six months was also twice the contract period for which Helga was employed, negotiated an extension of another three months, so when the day arrived Helga cried she would miss the baby and requested permission to come and visit him periodically.

My father left a written permission for Helga's entrance at the main gates of the Camp but her last day was also the last time we saw her. She disappeared completely. Vanished.

Before we left Germany we received a postcard from her with best wishes and informing she had moved to Hamburg and was working as a nanny for an American family.

The last heard from her was that she was invited by the American family to go together back to the USA. Which she did!

One Sunday somebody knocks the door; It was cold so we first put a cover on my back and went to see who was knocking the door so early.

Surprised I see in front of me the leader of that Egyptian family, Daniel.

-'Hullo – how are you?.

-'Fine and You?'

-'Please come in. It is so cold; what can we do for you early Sunday?

-'My family would like to make an offer for your shop'-

-'I need to talk to my wife'- answered Majer.

-'Is she home? '-asked Daniel, looking in a hurry.

-'Well she is at home and still sleeping. Our baby is still very young and cries at night; so when it is possible we sleep till later.' – said Majer.

-'But you can tell me and later I will discuss it with her'.

'-The business you have is composed of: rental rights of the shop, a regular registered business, the company has three partners and you have 54 percent. Stock needs to be evaluated and listed.

Except stock we would like to offer US$1.500 for your part. The negotiation with your existing partners we take responsibility'- Proposed Daniel.

'-Mr Gatelli, I need first to talk to my wife and then to my partners to see if we can negotiate my part. I can anticipate to you that total stock market value is about US$10.000'-answered Majer –' but now I cannot answer; later I will talk to Roza and in the evening to my partners. Then we could meet.

-'Majer I wait for you at Abe´s Caffe in front of cabin 10?'-

-Daniel I'll be there tomorrow at 10 hrs'- and offered to shake his hand which he accepted immediately; we smiled at each other and Daniel left.

Majer sat in the kitchen´s stool and laid backwards on the wall to calm down a backache that just started and began thinking that selling his part in the silver ware business would automatically mean t leave Germany and go to Bolivia, start a new life faraway from wars, shootings and killings.

He decided to wait until Roza woke up and then talk to her. Majer started to get excited about travelling, new frontiers; a new life.

Go to Bolivia!

I learnt at the Camp's bookstore that they spoke Spanish and Aymara. Main cities were at a geographical height with La Paz being at 4.000 meters over sea level.

Did not have wars going on and very few Jews live or have lived there. Most migrants are from neighboring countries such as Peru, Chile and since WW2 various families moved from Europe.

Roza walked in and said she wanted to talk;

-'It is true that there are no wars, European style, in Bolivia. But there are hundreds of shootings during a month due to the various revolutions that occur periodically. I know you are now in friendly relations with some political leaders and military officers but they are the main cause of the daily shooting.

It´s dangerous and as you promised in Foerhrenwald I want my family out of Bolivia-' said Roza annoyed with the situation,

-'I have been working on this matter and although our shop with the partners improved a lot and is getting businesses from the Americans and leaving a reasonable surplus.

As you know we sell silver artifacts mainly produced in European installations; whenever there an officer returning home he buys these highly decorative and fashionable silver objects to take home and resell for a fortune. In Munich they don't have much cash so they pay in cigarettes, chocolate bars, women stockings and watches.

We do not sell this but we trade it for animal skin, leather and sell large quantities to smugglers. That is how the wheel turns; lately it has been turning too much and I also sense things could worsen.

I have an idea of where to go: quiet, some Jews live there, Spanish is the language and there a market gossip that the government there will open a free Zone to import without duties just to generate jobs and incentivate tourism and industry. The place is called Arica and when we came from Germany we rested and stayed a few days there'- Said majer.

-'I remember and I liked it' – said Roza.

A few days ago that Mizrahi called Daniel came to see me at the shop and after some friendly chat he said he (maybe other partners too) he had an offer for our silver business and proposed to purchase all my shares and my proportional participation on our stocks.

You are the first person I am telling about this deal. What do you think? –' finished Majer'.

-'We have had a reasonable life but we cannot have a normal family in a country with nice leaders, friendly people and excessively romantic that they are prepared to give their lives and those of their families and neighbors for an ideological and political cause' – said Roza and ended saying -'I respect heroes but do not want to be one'-.

The shop was sold and paid.

Majer went to Arica stayed one week in a simple hotel at the lower part of calle dieciocho. This was year 1953 .November.

His daughter Hinde was born in April,1954.

On April,24th,1955 we celebrated Hinde first anniversary arriving in Arica, Chile; very tired after a long train journey.

This is version number 1.

The story I believe most. To have the whole picture it was written next chapter. For version 2 (destination unknown) it is time wise very short (it starts with Roza and Majer deciding to go to Bolivia and Majer having a psychedelic trip.

10-DESTINATION UNKNOWN

Going back to April,1949, while living in the Foehrenwald Camp and as a sequence to the migrations to Israel done by Wolf and Haim; my parents, Majer and Roza, decided to follow them and go to Israel; immediately started to pack things. First they decided to send trunks and packages with silver artifacts so as to start a small business selling these in the Tel Aviv collectors markets.

Five trunks full of medium and small size artifacts were properly packed and shipping organized for delivery at Wolf´s home address and Haim`s as a backup. The shipping company would pick up the trunks at the Camp in a few days. We were going to see the travel agent by the end of the month so as to make reservations to travel to Israel.

Then the letter written by my uncle Wolf arrived. Written in Yiddish it was very conservative, greeting everybody here and inquiring on the health of grandma Szjandla. Telling us that both, Wolf and Haim, and respective families were well and in good health.

It continued:

"I regret to tell you that there is a war going on here between Jews from all over the world and millions of Arabs.

Their leader, The Mufti from Jerusalem, has called for holy war; to expel all foreigners, especially the Jews, from Arabia. If necessary exterminate them. No need to tell you that the Mufti was considered a sympathizer of Hitler´s ideas.

We are living in fear with the children protected in a Kibbutz. Just want to ask for your help to handle things so that we can leave Israel and go to the United States. Here we cannot work as tailors and to continue working as peasants will not allow us to survive and we will probably never learn to do it properly.

Please do what you can and help us go to USA. I write this letter in my name and Haim`s.

Best wishes from your brother Wolf'.

The letter exploded like a bomb.

My mother read it in tears, that night at the Foerhenwald, and after a few minutes crying and complaining, she decided:

-'I am pregnant, I just left a war behind, I want to constitute a family and live in peace. We shall not go to Israel. Not in wartime. Let´s get back our five trunks. Let´s go somewhere else without war'. Anywhere!

So they started wandering about and asking people where to go.

My father would meet DPs daily at a Coffee House in Franz Joseph Strasse and hear the news and gossips.

Very soon we had answer considering our conditions: limited resources to pay for a visa, outside of Europe, Jewish community available, no wars.

From available information the region that could satisfy us and our selection criteria was South America.

-'They spoke mainly Spanish so we will go back to school? - asked my mother smiling.

We talked with other families that we found out also declined from travelling to Israel due to the same reason, war. As a result from these conversations we searched for a country in South America which would facilitate visas for us.

We tried Brazil and Argentina and rapidly got a negative answer. The main reason being, poor Jews are not interesting. They said their countries had established quotas for immigration and these were already full.

There may be an additional quota to enter but to live in small towns. The main reason was the extra cost of the immigration visa.

It took a few months to discuss Chile and received a negative answer. Beginning of 1951 during a routine follow up with the consulates we got a positive answer from the assistant consul from Bolivia.

Actually we monitored all South American and North American countries for a quota or any type of positive answer.

My father and the other four head of families went to the Bolivian Consulate, had a meeting with the assistant Consul.

After some tough negotiation he charged five hundred US dollars per person. The visas would be available immediately after payment.

For those interested they would print the forms now and when they returned for payment, the signed and stamped visa would be available in minutes. Everybody filled in and signed the forms and placed their finger digitals at the bottom of the form.

In two days we had to come back with the five hundred American dollars per person (adult or child) and the visas would be issued on the spot.

We talked to some American administrators at the Camp and asked them if they knew about how life was in Bolivia.

One soldier-lawyer had been there but entered Bolivia from Brazil´s side. We were going to enter Bolivia from the Andes or the Pacific side. The Andes are a chain of mountains from Alaska, going down the Pacific Ocean shores, all the way down to Chile.

-'The entrance to Bolivia from the Brazilian side is pure jungle' –he said and after a pause continued:

-'Hot and humid like hell. But very natural and people are friendly.

There are many trees, many types of birds, wild animals, snakes and Piranhas in the rivers. That part of Bolivia is the only region I have been.

They have main cities up in the mountains. La Paz is placed on the mountains at three thousand six hundred meters over sea level and you need to get used to live at that height. There are many Europeans and Americans living and working there.

Actually there is an American mission searching for fugitive Nazis that may have escaped Europe and consider themselves safe and protected in various countries in South America.

They did have some military and economic relationship during the WW2 and it was transformed into a protection scheme' – he made a new pause and the American continued,

-'Still, you will have more business opportunities there than here. People are naturally lazy, apparently, and you are used to hard work'. Then stopped for a pause.

-'Are you guys married?' – He asked.

Everybody answered yes.

-'Well'- he said - 'where I went, Santa Cruz de la Sierra and Cochabamba, women are very nice and friendly with foreigners'.

-'They call us Gringos and they are furiously after our money'

The five where getting more comfortable with the idea of going from destroyed Europe to unknown Bolivia and confirmed we would all be at the consulate to pay the visa fees and get the documents for entry into Bolivia.

Someone said something like 'being one – eyed in s country of blind' because that is want they thought it would be.

-'How do we get there?'- Somebody remembered to ask

-'Let′s go in Munich into a travel agency'. So they did.

The manager of the travel agency informed that the port of departure would be Genova, Italy.

The next vessel was the Antoniotto Usodimare and its next departure was scheduled for 35 days ahead.

-'Ideally you should arrive in Genova two or three days ahead' - He advised.

So we had some time to put things together, accept the offer to get rid of some of our belongings and try and learn about Bolivia.

My father′s immediate destination was the Camp′s library. Free and silent.

Before returning to find the person who intermediates the Bolivian visas he went to get information.

The library had a very large area with many large tables and individual chairs. I approached the librarian, an old man, and asked for any book in German about Bolivia.

He brought a pile of books; Geographical maps, History and legends of the Bolivian original peoples.

This last one interested my father because it was very small. Around fifty pages and had drawings and photos. It was called 'Origins of Man' - A Chiriguana people legend gathered by many storytellers during centuries.

In the Library it was so quiet, warm and relaxed that I started to read eagerly. Something I have not done for a long time.

Maybe in years.

The book's introduction started explaining that the Chiriguana people were from the Guarani branch, ethnic Guaranis that speak Tupi-Guarani and live in Bolivia near the border with Argentina and Paraguay.

Feeling relaxed and cozy he started reading that in the Chiriguana mythology two Gods govern the world.

Tumpaete who represents Good and Aguaratumpa represent evil. Both fight each other since the beginning of time and until the end of the days.

So it happened a long time ago, when Aguaratumpa the evil God, who knew well heaven and with his knowledge of Tumpaete, whom he had created and protected, made a mistake and caused a large fire that burnt all the plantations, the fields, the forests that belonged to the Chiriguanos and exterminated all the animals that lived there.

After crying for days the Chiriguanos decided to appeal to their God Tumpaete.

Tumpaete listened to their story and advised them to move their living houses to the riverside. And there they planted corn. While the corn plantation was growing they would feed on the fish from the river.

The Chiriguanos lived in large communal huts keeping up to one hundred individuals; several of these huts made up a village.

Aguaratumpa, the evil God, witnessing that his destructive effort was failing, made the skies rain so hard that everything was flooded; including all the corn fields that the Chiriguanos had planted.

Antropophagy was well disseminated and connected to the belief of taking over the power of the enemy. They ate whatever they could get from the land and animals they hunted. Even their enemies.

As results were not satisfactory, again the Chiriguanos went to talk to the God Tumpaete, the good God.

And Tumpaete spoke: 'It has been decided that you will all die drowned and to save your race you must find a large gigantic vase and inside leave two children. A male and a female, born to the same woman selected within the strongest and fittest; they will be the tree from which the new Chiriguana race will be born again.

The Chiriguanos obeyed their God of goodness.

Rain did not stop for many months and the gigantic vase with the children inside continued to float over the waters.

Everybody died, nobody survived. When God Aguaratumpa felt that the Chiriguano race had disappeared, he stopped the rain.

Now Aguaratumpa believed that he owned the earth.

The fields dried out and the sun came out to warm the fields and the forests. The two children in the vase that passed unnoticed, came out of their hideaway.

The couple walked and walked for a long time in search of food. They went from one side to the other, from left to right; and hunger started to cause pain. This was their messianic search for the "Land without Evil".

Then the Good God Tumpaete appeared again and spoke to them:

'Go in search of Cururu, the good friend of mankind. He will give you fire and with this fire you can cook the fish from the river.

The children walked without rest until they found Cururu seating in a high place. Burning coals were kept in his mouth and he kept them on fire with his breath.

He gave the burning coals to the children and they were able to cook the fish that were plentiful due to the big rains.

Cururu then told them that when the torrential rains started, following orders from Tumpaete, he dug himself into the center of the earth carrying the burning coals on fire in his mouth.

Thanks to that fire the children ate and survived.

Both, brother and sister, grew up with the years until they had the age to proliferate. From this couple, the Chiriguanos multiplied themselves and formed again a people robust, beautiful and perfect.

This story I had seen in colors and with some funny music in the back. Like a movie. "Wake up Sir" – said the voice standing next to me.

It was the library's attendant shaking Majer smoothly. He had slept using as head's support the book about the Chiriguanos. Did not read anything except the book's title and then started day dreaming. He was tired but the library's relaxed nap had freshened him up.

-'I do not believe in interpreting dreams but this one was different. I do not recall having dreams of exotic places, exotic people with exotic ideas. About religious subjects never. Will think about it' – Majerr told the story to Roza and Grandma – and finished- 'my original intention in going to the Public Library was to learn something about Bolivia, something practical, everyday life, its people, its food.

Meanwhile I slept on top of the book and dreamt a story that mixes world creation, Moses survival, Noah; and Good and Bad' – he finished.

Majer wanted to believe that his dream was a message that we would start a new life in Bolivia and maybe Cururu will have some fire for us.

Next day Majer found in the area we called 'living room' a trapped bird that somehow entered but frightened entered a frantic flight designed to escape capture and in the meantime was hurting himself bumping against the windows, the walls and some furniture.

Very calmly he walked to the window an opened it wide open; then walked back and stood up against the wall watching the small bird as it felt the open window and slowly found his way out. Suddenly it flew away and disappeared. Even for a small bird freedom is innate and an endless search. At the meeting place in Munich, having a coffee, a newcomer from Norway whose brother was in Foerhenwald was telling stories about Norway.

We did not receive much news from his homeland except in special events and this was one.

He was just arriving at the Camp with his family and we were leaving to Genova by bus, from Genova to Arica by ship and from there by train to La Paz.

Anxiety was in each finger tip.

11-CHANGE OF PLANS

Going back in this story and to keep its horizon in sight we had:

Wolf and Haim had been already in Israel since the beginning of 1948.

Soon after they arrived they found out there was a war for the creation of a Jewish State; the so called War of Independence.

Most immigrants went to live in community run organizations called Kibbutzim and most adults were trained to shoot and fight.

At the Camp Foehrenwald, there were two kibbutzim with the intention to prepare Jews to work the land, provide occupation for those searching for a job and willing and produce agricultural goods. It also helped to create a friendlier atmosphere and for sure prepared soldiers for Israel (or mandate Palestine while it was in the hands of the British).

The children were separated from their parents during daytime and had monitors for learning Hebrew, other subjects, eat and play. Only at night they saw their parents for a short time. The children slept with their colleagues. Seemed too military but actually it was very convenient, if you look at it from the point of view of work to be done at the Kibbutz and security services all day and night.

Adults also had Hebrew lessons. Every person considered an adult was trained in the art of self defense and use of arms. Their apparent intention was to create a unified people speaking a common language, Hebrew. Yiddish seemed to bother them although represented its past and present. Probably for the future, except the orthodox, Yiddish will be a half dead language.

At this kibbutz training centers they taught the children only Hebrew songs. No Yiddish, No Ladino.

In May, 1948, the neighboring Arab countries tried to occupy all the lands granted by the United Nations to the future Jewish state called Israel, and the Israelis reacted starting a war in various simultaneous fronts .This reaction was called the War of Independence and in defense of their survival, that the English colonial power instead of being peace mediator, decided to abandon its former colonial territories in Palestine to its destiny. It was said that the Mufti of Jerusalem declared in favour of the destruction of the just born state of Israel.

People had already written letters in Israel to be sent to family and friends living in Europe telling about a new war in Israel and invasion by the Arabs with war material left by the British, that very quickly decided to leave the area.

Obviously, restrictions started with ammunition, food, water and others. It was not a state priority to build an economy and give incentives for commerce and local production. Their worry summarized to one word: Survival!

The letters that Majer received from his brothers and letters that other Camp dwellers received, were full of negative comments and the future did not seem to be bright. They told stories of people being killed by bullets, knifed by suicide attackers, water wells being poisoned and camels too. The letters also mentioned food rationing and nights without sleep. Things were very hard on women and children.

The feeling in the Camp Foehrenwald was that this new war, in the middle east would last forever and, in general, the world did not care about the future of the Jewish communities and probably less about a Jewish state. So why go there?

There was a group of people with an Idealistic view of Israel. The Zionists, they dreamt with a life of plenty in Israel; Biblical homeland of the Jewish nation, Land of King David.

The hearts and minds of the majority of Jews in Europe were set on immigrating to Israel. It was a centuries old communal wish and the Nazi Empire showed that something was deeply wrong with Europe.

They, most European countries, accepted Hitler's impositions easily, that even when losing their independence and becoming slave states, I would somehow suspect, they would have accepted a Unified Nazi Europe. Germany and Austria were the original Nazis; Italy with its own dictator, Benito Mussolini, already had become a second class partner.

Russia at the beginning of WW2 was an ally of Germany thru a non- aggression pact. Many other countries preferred a passive status and just observed what was happening in Europe. England without Sir Winston Churchill would be eager to stay out or join the Nazis in a non-aggression pact.

Thanks to Sir Winston Churchill's resilience and stubbornness, WW2 was redirected with the USA totally involved, from this point onwards the war was won.

If it the result would have been different?

What would have happened to the European Jews? They would have disappeared in a worldwide effort by Nazi Germany and its allies. What happens next?

For sure Jews in Europe (Nazi Europe) would have disappeared, literally speaking, they would have been incinerated. Germany again would sign no aggression pact with the Soviet Union, the eventual danger for the Nazis would be established in North and South America.

North America, meaning the United States of America, kept herself isolated from the war until the Pearl Harbor attack.

They really made a difference, and eventually South America followed the USA because of the American economical influence, war incentives; although some countries had sympathy for Hitler's regime. Really, the war was declared between the USA and Japan, by the Japanese, thru the bombing of naval installations of the USA in the Pacific region.

The Arab countries respected the opinion of the Mufti of Jerusalem, a deep hearted Anti-Jewish well known Arab leader with a pro-Nazi bias.

While 'on the winning streak', Germany had a lot of sympathy from most countries; and with regards to the Jewish Question, well, it was a problem that Nazi Germany thought knew how to solve definitively. They developed their own know- how.

What the Holy Inquisition was not able to do in a few hundred years, the Germans nearly did in six years.

Japan decided to test their strategies by attacking Pearl Harbor and Germany decided to emulate Napoleon by invading Russia.

These disturbed people decided to poke powerful forces hidden in some countries and they found a strong will and resources in the USA and an iron fist in England.

Let´s go back to our intentions in departing Europe.

Trunks with silver objects and other items had already been sent to Haim´s address in Israel.

These objects belonged to Majer and Roza and meant an important part of their accumulated capital and savings since the end of World War II.

Sent and gone. My father was supposed to try and recover these trunks. He tried and was not successful. The transport company confirmed it had shipped the trunks.

It informed the delivery at Haim´s address in Israel but nobody was available there to receive the goods. So the responsible for delivery left the trunks at the Kibutz´s entrance from where they disappeared.

Start again and at the same time put responsibility on the delivery company. Majer had the feeling that he already knew this situation of hopelessness. But need to fight against it, so started again to work to put together some money and goods. The question now is where to go?

A few months went on and together with some colleagues they traded with the Americans and the Germans; until one day a comrade from the Foehrenwald Camp asked him if he was interested in migrating to South America; specifically to Bolivia. There was no food shortage, no war, similar weather and needed more people to grow.

Majer said he was interested and they arranged to meet in a few days at the Bolivian Consulate in Munich. Meanwhile he walked into the bookshop of the Camp and asked the attendant for information about Bolivia.

He brought a large book with maps and showed that of South America and pinpointed Bolivia´s location. It was green, no seaside and mixed mountains with jungle.

The economical capital, La Paz, was high in the mountain´s area. He thanked the attendant and asked,

-'How do we get to La Paz?': -'From Munich to St Gallen and from there south in the direction of Liechtenstein'; 'from there to Bellinzona' - and continued – 'and then a quick stop on the city of Como on the shore of the lake with the same name and finally to Genova.

In Genova you can take the ship that travels to the Pacific Coast of Chile.' – answered the attendant.

-'Ok, many thanks; another question' – Majer said- 'which port would be our destination?'

-'Let me see in the map; Arica' - said the attendant and continued trying to be as friendly as possible –'It says in the small print in English that there is three times a week a train service between the arrival port of Arica, and La Paz, your final destination in Bolivia.'

-'Does it say anywhere if La Paz is a jungle? With wild animals?' – asked Majer.

-'No, on the contrary, it is the main economical center and is located in the mountains at four thousand two hundred and sixty five meters over the sea level, for the El Alto airport and the only big animals are the Llamas'.

Majer asked for the cost of the map book. 'Ten dollars' - he answered. It was too expensive so he planned to bring my mother to the Bookshop to see for herself. But first, needed to discuss the acceptability of Bolivia. So he went home, DP Camp, and asked his wife if everything was in order and received a yes as an answer.

-'Change of plans' – My father said smiling to my mother.

-'What?' – She answered

-'Change of plans! We do not go to Israel anymore' – Majer said.

-'OK, But I don´t want to live in Europe. There will be new wars, new Progroms, new persecutions.' – said Roza.

-'Yes, We have a change of plans! We will go to Bolivia!' – said Majer.

-'Where? Bolivia? In the middle of the jungle?' –asked Roza.

-'No, in the mountains! To La Paz!'

-'What is La Paz? Who else from the Camp is going? Are there Jews over there? Is there at least a Minyam?'- questioned mother.

-'Do not know. Will ask around; Rabbi Fischer probably knows somebody and how things are there' – answered my father.

The trip from Foehrenwald, Germany to Genoa, Italy, was supposed to last around fifteen hours. Two small buses were rented with two drivers each.

The passengers were eight families and a total of thirty five persons.

The road distance was around six hundred and eighty five kilometers and according to the Camp's manager should be very interesting and different. We just went to say goodbye to the general manager of the Camp, an American Jewish Soldier whom, me and my brothers met when the Red Army troops and the American troops close the encirclement of Berlin.

About the DPs Camps, originally after the Allies invasion, in the USA zone they were planned for all DPs and with the clear order of General Patton to collect DPs and repatriate them back to their countries of origin.

This idea caused many complaints for obvious reasons.

Patton's idea collapsed with his death. Immediately US commanders following senior orders modified the Camps having Munich area Camps been exclusively dedicated to Jews and the main Camps managed by US officers, mostly Jewish.

There were some families of German origin. These were Jewish survivors who survived the Holocaust and lived because they were married to Germans or were born of mixed marriages. In Bavaria almost one thousand Jews in this status survived.

Next day at 09 a.m. the buses started moving. We had packed all night and spent most part of the morning saying farewell to those neighbors and friends while crying of happiness.

We did not like the Camp but we knew we were going to miss it. Six years had gone there and many neighbors and friends.

The buses took the road to Rosenheim (Bavaria) where in the destroyed city a return to life of a football team the year before was still commemorated in the streets. It was the TSV 1860 Rosenheim. We went thru it very rapidly.

Then continued in the direction of the Alps and passed thru the ancient city of Berchtesgarden also destroyed by the American Airforce in 1945 but rapidly being reconstructed.

Nearby was the so called Hitler's Mountain, the Odersalzberg.

Next was Innsbruck, a ski center very famous and preferred by the well- known and rich people. We stopped for coffee and cake in a downtown Plaza.

The waiter was very interested in our trip. He was married to a Jewish girl. He told us that the city and the area had suffered many avalanches, more than six hundred and fifty in a period of three months, and that there were more than two hundred persons killed. It was raining for weeks and continued to rain.

We had a meeting and decided to spend the night in a small hotel in the outskirts of town, available, clean and cheap.

Next day at 08 a.m. we were on the road again.

The direction was to Italy and the closest city in a road plan was Bolzano, then Trento and finally Rovereto. The whole region was flooded, so bus speed was very slow and careful. From the three old towns, Trento was the best known.

Now in 1951 for the floods, named the Polesine flood and in history for Catholic Church Council of Trento in the Middle Ages which lasted for many years (1539-1562).

In Rovereto we found a nice small hotel and decided to eat and spend the night there. Next day it was going to be our last part of the trip and ought to leave us in Genoa at nighttime. Close was the Lake Garda.

Departed at 08 a.m. destination Brescia in the Province of Lombardy, in the Alps region. The city was from old Roman origin, called the "Lioness of Italy" and in modern times an industrial center.

Cremona was next, in a mixed Lombardy and Emilia region, a city cut by three rivers; Adda, Oglio and Po. Although Italian it had a Germanic look. Maybe because it´s Austrian relationship.

After a longer period without entering a town we arrived, in Tortola, a small city in the region of Piemonte with old Roman heritage.

Only seventy six kilometers from our final destination. Finally two hours later we were arriving in front of the Hotel in Genova, main city and port of the region of Liguria.

Some say the city of origin of Christopher Columbus, the man that discovered the New World in 1492 with three sailing vessels, financed by Spain´s Catholic monarchs who themselves self-financed all needs with confiscated goods and valuables

We had three days before the ship`s departure and decided to visit part of Liguria. I was told by other travelling Jews that the port city of La Spezia was the main point of departure of Jews, Italian and others, from Italy to Mandate Palestine, Israel.

We all booked in a small and simple hotel near the port and kept the buses for another three days.

When considering this trip we must consider the children with us and state of our vehicles that quite often had to be maintained for dome mechanical part and most important the state of the roads that in some cases just did not exist.

Some were feeling homesick of their camp barracks and some admiring the sights during the day and getting anxious to go on the ship;

12- IN ITALY

La Spezia was a small city on the Mediterranean Sea and a maritime port. Jews left Italy from there during the WW2 years and after the war too.

Fascist Italy had also its stories of intolerance and antisemitism. In 1938 the "Racial Laws" were issued and implemented in 1940 segregating Jews born in Italy and those not born in Italy.

Later the Jews born in Italy were segregated again by separating and interning in concentration Camps the "Dangerous" Jews with 'regards to their capacity for defeatist propaganda and espionage activities'.

So if you were depressive you go imprisoned.

Officially Italy joined Nazi Germany in is policy of elimination of the Jewish people when it issued the "Carta de Verona" on November,14th,1943; it was a Political manifesto making it legal the extermination of the Jews pursued by the Fascist regime. Before this behavior correction imposed by the German Gestapo, Italy seemed like a 'temporary heaven'.

La Spezia was a relative short drive, the small buses we had rented were reasonably comfortable and the drivers very friendly.

From La Spezia we went to see Cinque Terre and we stopped at Monterosso al Mare, a tiny fisherman's town full with flowers in the house's balconies.

Both La Spezia and Monterosso are for walking and for us was difficult since Grandma had difficulties, she complained most of the time that her legs were hurting and that she was hungry. It was lunch time!

The drivers took us to a small restaurant where they knew the owner, a Jew.

He said it in a way as we would really appreciate his choice. After seating in a larger table, the owner came to take the order and the driver whispered in his ear. He said to us that the owner wanted to speak with us. He knew some Yiddish and some German so he could manage.

His point of interest was how did the family survive Nazi Germany?

I told him, speaking very slowly and mechanically, a summary of our stories, runaway from home, bunker hiding, join the Red Army, change sides, live in Foehrenwald, get married, have a child, depart from Europe.

The restaurant's owner had already pushed a chair near us and joined at the table; called his wife to help and join us. He wanted confirmation of the concentration and extermination Camps and shed a few tears smoothly when the stories were told.

He had heard about these camps but did not accept it as possible. How could they? How could anyone have even tried? These were some of the questions put on the table.

Then with a glass of red wine, sweet wine for the ladies, he insisted in having information of the Red Army and the defeat of the Germans.

I told him that me and my brothers had abandoned Poland, walked into Russia and joined the army after leaving one younger brother with our mother, to hide in a farm's bunker in the forest.

In Russia we had a very quick military training, got winter clothes, boots and a rifle.

In a few months we changed from being attacked and defending ourselves from the Nazis to attacking them. Basically did not stop moving ahead until we reached the outskirts of Berlin.

Destroyed Berlin and together with the American forces took over after being successful in a gigantic encirclement operation that killed and imprisoned thousands of enemy soldiers. As soon as possible we managed to crossover to the American Zone and requested to be admitted in a DPs Camp near Munich. Meanwhile we could not forget the thousands of dead bodies of teenagers and children spread out on the fields. For days we have been receiving information about youngsters being use in the defense of Munich and nearby towns. But now we were seeing them. This subject, I explained to my friend seating at the table of the Italian Restaurant was my personal hell at nighttime;

The owner, already acquainted with most of us, served the fish and salads and sat down again at our table and looking in the eyes of some of us asked bluntly:

-'Is Hitler alive? Because in Italy they say he is alive and hiding. In a few years he will take back Germany and start the Reich again'.

I told him I did not know for sure. War is very confusing. Still I believed what we heard at the Red Army, and later with the American soldiers, that he, his lover and other big shots of the Nazi regime, had committed suicide instead of falling in the hands of the Russians, said that he was caught by the Russians and taken to Moscow.

We continued eating and drinking while the restaurant owner satisfied his anxiety for news from WW2.

Before driving back to Genova we decided do have diner in an Italian Trattoria in La Spezia and having been recommended by a taxi driver we drove to Il Lupo Ristorante. We all entered the main saloon and sat on a long table. Being so many called the attention of the waiter, who called the manager who happened to be also the owner.

-'Giuseppe Brindise at your orders'- he said in a broken German after he heard us speaking Yiddish between us.

-'Piaccere'- We greeted with the Italian word'- We would like to have diner. It is a special occasion; our last night in Europe'- We answered in German.

-'Why?'- Giuseppe asked.

-'We are embarking in a ship in Genova tomorrow and will depart to Port of Arica in the north of Chile; then by train to our final destination: La Paz, Bolivia.'

-'OK, Let`s find out what do you want to eat and drink and then we can talk more'- said the owner.

After some twenty minutes, Giuseppe had taken the complete order and ordered the waiters to put bread, butter, virgin olive oil and olives on the table for everybody.

-' Water, soft drinks on the house, and also one bottle of red wine' – he instructed his assistant.

Everybody was drinking when Giuseppe came for a toast;

-' Bon Voyage, Salute!'- He said loudly.

He sat at the head of the table near us and said:

-'I can see you are all Jewish. Where are you from?'

-'Basically born in Poland and lately spend a few years at a DP Camp in Germany, called Foerhenwald near Munich'. Most of the children were born at the Camp.'

-'My family is also Jewish, from Genova. We have been in Italy for centuries and during the war we decided to move to La Spezia and start again . opening this restaurant. I am sorry we are not kosher. Are you?' – asked Giuseppe.

-'Not religious but we would like to avoid having seafood with the pasta' – somebody answered.

He quickly called the waiter and gave the orders to avoid totally seafood. But fish was OK.

-'Did you run a restaurant before and during the war, Mr. Giuseppe?'- asked Majer.

-'My family owned a restaurant in Genova. I helped whenever possible but my profession was Professor of History at the University of Genoa.

When the war started with the occupation of Poland in 1939, I was lecturing at the University. When the German Army and SS, came into Italy all Jewish University professors were dismissed. From one day to another we were left with no jobs, no salary and with the possibility of going to jail if we protested because of our situation.

Suddenly the fascist became Nazis.

Nobody worried about Jews before. Now they were receiving orders to segregate Jews, to limit selected areas for living quarters, to be expelled from public jobs.

So I took my wife and children and came to Genoa where I thought we could have a quiet time and let the war pass' – answered Giuseppe looking in the kitchen's direction.

-'How many Jews lived in Italy before the war?' – One of us asked.

-'About Eighty thousand'-answered Giuseppe. – 'Initially those not born in Italy were rounded up and transported to camps in Germany and Austria.

Then those "oriundi' but with political participation'.

We all had heard that Italians refused to send Jews to the extermination camps and some facilitated the disappearance of the Jewish people but many obeyed the German's instructions and orders'.

-'Not so many Jews in Italy; in Poland we were three and half million and after the war we were left around three hundred and fifty thousand or less, if we include those returned by the Russians' - I commented.

-'Did Italy have many Jews migrating to Israel, United States or other countries?' – asked one of us.

-'Let me remember my days of professor of history and talk about the Jews in Italy, OK? – inquired Giuseppe.

-'Yes please, but talk slowly so we can understand better'- Roza advised. '-Your German language is very good but remember we speak Yiddish and also understand German'- said I.

-'OK, Will do my best'. But first let me try to answer your question about Jewish emigration from Italy.

To the United States it has been many years since Italians started migration. They say there are over 1 million Italians in New York. To Israel a few Zionists young people full of ideals and older people that basically want to be buried there' – lectured Giuseppe.

He took his glass of wine and drank half of it, then like if he was giving a lecture in the University:

-'The presence of Jewish people in Italy goes back more than two thousand years, when Rome was an Empire and the Holy Land, Israel, one of its colonies.

Colonial relations were very positive and old documents showed that Israel and Rome had an alliance to defend each other against the Seleucid Kingdom.

In those years, Jews and Greeks came to Rome as merchants or slaves. The Romans did not have a high appreciation of the Jewish faith but respected it as an old religion and the famous Jerusalem`s temple.

Jews acted differently than now with respect to their religion. They were very active in proselytizing the local Romans into Judaism. This way the number of converts into Judaism grew. In this period the Christian faith was inexistent.

Here we should make a short stop and say a few words about a famous Jewish-Roman personality: The historian known as Flavius Josephus, his Jewish name was Joseph ben Mattathias. A citizen of Rome, lived from around 37 AC until 100 AC. In these years he was a witness of the so called "Jewish Wars" participating first on Israel´s side as a General defending Galilee against the troops of Vespasian. He was defeated and defected to the Roman side where he became an adviser to Roman general Vespasian and his son Titus. Both Romans became Emperors of the Roman Empire.

While with the Romans, Josephus became friends with Titus who took him to Rome. During his years in Rome he always managed to have a protector and lived as an aristocrat and historian, writing various books.

He remained in the limelight until the murder of Emperor Domitian, then he faded away. This shows only one aspect of the integration that went on.

Many Jews that lived outside Israel assimilated into the Roman Empire`s culture, especially those living in the large cities.' - Giuseppe stopped to ask for another bottle of red wine and said to the waiter it was on the house.

-'Christianity became a legal religion of the Roman Empire 300 AC. The Emperor that brought this new religion to the public of the Empire was Constantine in 313 AC and immediately started to make life difficult for the Jewish population.

Two hundred years later, in the 500s AC, there were many Jewish communities in what is known today as Italy. There were in Rome, Milan, Genoa, Palermo and other places. Apparently in this period the Jews did not suffer great persecutions' - Giuseppe made a pause.

-'Do you trace back your family to this time?'- asked one of my friends.

-'No, not so far back but 300 years after Christ, yes'- Answered Giuseppe and after he drank a mouthful of red wine he continued,

-'In the period from antiquity till the Middle Ages, around year 1200 nothing notorious happened that I can remember. Except the Crusades'- continued Giuseppe.

In the early Middle Ages actually happened the first international social movement with the open intention to recover Jerusalem, the Crusades and from many cities Jews were expelled, as example from Bologna in 1172 where Jews lived in peace.

A Jew with rabbinical family history was the property manager for Pope Alexander III.

The main question about the crusades was to recover the holy land and the holy places. Obviously, not for restoration of the land to the Jewish people.

But, for appropriation of the various kingdoms and to charge entrance fees for the visits to the holy places. The crusaders had most probably in their view the appropriation of lands owned and ruled by the Arabs.

Also interesting was the business of relics, booming in Europe and handled mainly by crusaders belonging to the religious-military orders.

Although there were many laws with measures against Jews they were ignored frequently in Italy. For sure in part due to their Latin temperament and to the fact that they were longtime neighbors.

Those Jews not born in Italy, therefore non-Italian Jews, did not have many defenders. Also during the crusades there probably were not Italian preachers. The first crusade whose period was from 1096 till 1099 was a disaster for the Jewish communities that lived on the "road to Jerusalem".

Three preachers remained in history, Peter the Hermit, Walter Sans Avoir and Folkmar.

Some historians called this crusade the first Holocaust because while

Marching thru cities (especially in France and Germany) Jews were forced to convert or die. Not exclusively conversion but also robbery and extortion of money from the frighten communities.

The conquest and retaking of Jerusalem by the Christian crusaders was a massacre of Jews and Muslims. Jews that were religious run into the synagogues for safety. These were locked from the outside and burnt to the ground.

There were various crusades but the one that remained in the books are the so called first crusade let by King Baldwin of Bourgogne, that succeeded in taking Jerusalem and the second crusade that lost Jerusalem to the Muslims, led by two kings Louis VII from France and Conrad III from Germany. Its period was from 1145 till 1149.

The head preacher, selected personally by the Pope, was Bernard de Clairvaux who caused also, thru his excited preaching, the murder of many Jews in their marching to Jerusalem. The Pope was very upset since he had a special appreciation for the Jewish people considering that some worked for him taking care of medical matters and finances.

Many Jews held important functions such as property managers, treasury and physicians.

Also in the Arts, poets and religious experts, specialist translators worked in the translation and interpretation of Arab astronomy.

Under Pope Innocent conditions for Jews worsened in Italy. He created the yellow arm badge that every Jew had to wear.

Other Popes behaved similarly and these attitudes, and the anti-Jewish environment, continued until the 1500s.

In this new period a more pragmatic mentality started to takeover and people in power understood that commercial interests were more important than religious affairs.

Jews grew as bankers, merchants and financial advisors to the rich and powerful. In parallel, Jews became well known physicians and this gave them higher status.

When Spain decided to expel the Jews in 1492 also Sicily and Naples, both dominated by Spain, ordered the expulsion of Jewish people too.

The effective application of these rules was very slow but it happened. In the second half of the 16th century Jews from Venice and Rome migrated to Poland and Lithuania.

In a typical Latin confusion some Jews were going and at the same time others were coming; especially those expelled from Spain at procuring refuge and protection in Naples, Ferrara, Tuscany.

At the same time they were made to suffer in Rome and Genova.

Special times: While the Catholic Monarchs in Spain were totally committed to the expulsion or conversion of the Jewish community; the Papal States accepted and welcomed these Jews' – Stopped Giuseppe his lecture.

-'I thought that Spain had been forced to expel the Jews with the total support of the Catholic Inquisition run by the Catholic Church in Spain and that this meant total support and incentives from the head of the church, the Pope' - one of the men asked.

-'It is a bit confusing but that is the nature of men. First your personal interest then follow the community's'- answered Giuseppe.

This change in attitude brought with it a novelty: Jews were being forced to live in specially assigned areas that later became exclusive: the ghettos.

The Inquisition that was commanded by the equivalent to the ultra conservative part of society, the most conservative segment of society, tried always to work its way thru the most crowded cities. Crowded with Jews!

During the 16th century there were many expulsions decrees on various subjects that were constantly used by the Anti-Semites: The Talmud was blamed for being dangerous, teaching the practice of ritual murder and so on.

One tolerant Pope is followed by another intolerant Pope. The arrival of intolerance normally caused that Jews would leave again to yet another new city or convert to Catholicism after being exhausted of running away from anti-Semite cities.

The city of Venice was shaken by the nomination of the Turkish Empire, as Ambassador to Venice, of a well-known Jew from Constantinople; Solomon of Udine; in 1574. The Venetian Senate had approved an expulsion decree and now it was confronted with this Jewish Ambassador.

Venetian Society put pressure from various corners on the Senate and men with great influence in Venice were successful in revoking the expulsion decree. Ambassador Solomon had a very positive period in Venice and counted with the influence of very important men and their families. Some cities of Italy welcomed Jews, some did not.

This is one factor in favor of the thinking that anti-Judaism depended on the communities and their leaders and not necessarily on twisted minded individual people's actions.

This positive period was followed by some years where two Popes, Paul IV and Pious V produced decrees that humiliated the Jewish population and caused an exodus leaving just a few thousand Jews in Italy ' – paused Giuseppe after talking uninterruptedly for various minutes.

-'But what did these Popes do that humiliated Jews in those days?'- asked Majer.

'Well, many things. Such as: Jewish doctors were prohibited to assist Christian patients, Marrano Jews that come from Spain and Portugal could not be assisted or helped under the punishment of having to face the Holy inquisition intervene, burnt the Talmud and other religious books. Services for the conversion of Jews included in the daily church services, one third of the community was forced to be present, were forced to listen to these sermons in the synagogues. But as nothing lasts forever, the next Popes were a positive sign'.

-'They turned around most of the decrees. The Duchy of Milan was under Spanish rule and Jews were tolerated; inconsistency, that is at the end, very dangerous for Jews. Why dangerous? Because the Jewish people accommodated hoping, and believing, that finally they found a place where they could live, raise their children and work and study in peace' -said Giuseppe and continued – 'Then things calmed down'.

The Popes that came in sequence granted various demands from the Jewish communities; like permission to reprint the Talmud and other religious books. In parallel there were actions to convert Jews, books and lectures for preaching to the Jews of Rome.

Then appeared Napoleon Bonaparte, who introduced a liberal religious policy and under his influence the Jews in Italy were emancipated. The power yielded by the Popes was broken. Many positive actions were taken and Jewish communities were never before so free.

But this freedom lasted very little. It disappeared together with Napoleon's power. Again we had back medieval servitude and improvement of conditions for the Jews, had to wait.

During the unification of the states to create a unified Italy, many Jews fought for unification and others distinguished themselves in various activities. Many assisted important Italian public personalities and also many occupied high level government positions.

At the beginning of this century, in 1910, a Jew called Luigi Luzzatti took office as Italy's prime minister and another Jew, Ernesto Nathan was Rome's mayor from 1907 till 1913. These were practicing Jews with the Jewish faith, not converted or crypto Jews.

Some commentator of Papal actions and thoughts said that the Vatican kept hidden for some time their definition of Anti-Judaism and its attitudes and there were two: the good and the bad' – said Giuseppe in a lecturer's mood.

-'Can it be that they believe in good Anti-Judaism? Good Hitler?'- Someone at the table asked.

-'The good Anti-Judaism denounced plots apparently for the purpose of gaining control of the world by controlling newspapers, banks, schools, etc.

The bad Anti-Judaism was that directed hate merely because of their descent.

This document was the guidance on Anti-Judaism practiced by the Church in the 19 and 20th century' – answered Giuseppe showing signs of being tired.

'-Giuseppe, many thanks for your interesting lecture.

We all have learnt a lot about Italy and the Jews. But before we go I think we would be very interested in a short story of how the Italians behaved during the WW2 especially in relation to the Jewish people'- Majer Mr. Giuseppe.

Worried about choosing the words, Giuseppe started:

-'Before the WW2 Italy already was living in a right wing political system called Fascism. Influenced by Nazism it promoted the superiority of races and was against communism and bourgeois capitalism.

Only in 1938 the fascist regime commanded by Mussolini issued the racial laws. Some high status figures of the Catholic Church condemned racism and made it known publically.

Before these laws, Jews participated in the National Fascist Party and held high positions in government and private companies. When Italy entered the war, in 1940, Jewish refugees were placed in concentration Camps. In many cases Italian commanders refused to deliver the Jews to their German partners and also did not cooperate with sending them to extermination Camps.

When Italy capitulated to the North American troops, in 1943, the Germans in response invaded Italy from the North. The Nazis searching desperately for Jews in the concentration Camps found surprises: from the Campagna concentration Camp all Jews had fled to the mountains with the help of the locals.

Still out of a population of forty five thousand before the war, around ten thousand became victims of the Nazi hysteria. They were mostly originated in the Ghettos of Rome, Genoa and Florence and others. Most were assassinated in Auschwitz.

Although the death of one innocent person for any reason is a major crime Italians avoided sending Jews to the German extermination Camps as long as it was possible. They disobeyed orders or destroyed them until 1943 after the German invasion.

Excluded from Italian society by the laws that Mussolini issued forbidding Jewish children to attend school, public or private, dismissed for university as professors or students and banned from military and civil service; the members of the community started immigrating to the USA mainly and other various countries'- Ended Giuseppe and asked the waiter to bring a few cards and on them wrote his name, address and postal direction.

He asked my father to write to him when established in Bolivia and hopefully one day he said he would visit them and bring back the memories of this pleasant afternoon.

Next day was departure day. Everybody was tired and at the same time excited and anxious for tomorrow to come. In this travelling we have made closer friends and got to know better the people that cohabitated with us at the Camp. Although a relatively short time it has been very intense in knowledge and making friends, I believe they call "fellow traveler" or "ship brother" those people that travel together by sea.

It becomes a sort of special brotherhood and in principle, like being brothers, it is forever.

Some of these brothers we never saw again and a few we saw often enough to review old travelling memories, funny events, dangerous moments and very happy "get together".

Grandma spent this travelling time amazed with the various environments we went thru. She watched for hours the mountains, the snowy peaks and the lakes. Enjoyed the ride she had for the first time and did not complain much. Except food, she was always in doubt about being kosher even when Majer guaranteed that everything they gave her to eat was strictly kosher.

She kept home, in Foehrenwald, kosher and supervised my mother's cooking. Kosher and way to cook were her specialties and when awake she would try to command everything going on in the kitchen.

Majer was worried about Grandma's future behavior in Bolivia. It was going to be difficult to keep kosher. He did not mind much but Grandma and Roza made a point in keeping home kosher and keeping all traditions as they learned from their parents and older generations.

I believe women suffer more than men when their roots are unearthed. They seem to have more connection with the human ground and when transplanted they take a longer time to accommodate their roots to a new soil. Many positive events must occur until the let go and keep the older memories in a separate compartment and open a new one for the new chance in life.

Knowing that others suffered more than we did, made us humble and grateful.

During our travelling we managed to hear various stories and concluded that ours was not so tough. It was not easy to take a ship to an unknown country with people that speak other language; that have different traditions and were used to different tastes and smells. Poor Grandma it was going to be, for sure, very traumatic for her.

She never said a word about her deceased husband but I could feel she missed him during the day and sometimes looked out the window as if she was waiting for her husband to come home.

She looked a few minutes, closed her eyes as in prayer and whispered something that seemed to be "I miss you, please come home". In a way she was very strong minded but physically exhausted.

Her hands trembled, she normally forgot where she left something and spent a long time searching until she or somebody found it and then got annoyed because she thought they were hiding things from her; had difficulties in performing simple tasks, sometimes remained with apathy without focus and had communication problems; she changed mood rapidly and for no apparent reason, and most of the time, she had difficulties in finding the right words.

All above plus some pain here and there and that she spoke only Yiddish and Polish made relations with her very complicated and most people simply avoided her.

Roza always repeated that when Grandma was younger and healthier she was a great cook of traditional Ashkenazi food.

She only went to Jewish School until twelve years old. This was considered modern when she was a child. Did not go to public school and learnt to read and write in Polish with her brothers.

She looked and dressed like a gypsy and was normally very kind to us but always had discussions, each in her own language, with the nanny and maid.

She also gave a hard time to anyone coming to our cabin in the camp; our temporary home. She wanted to know, who that was?. She discussed that person′s origin and complained to strangers that she was being mistreated and kept starving.

She also complained to visitors about her being a slave and having no valid opinion in the family affairs.

That was my Grandma!

13 - ACT OF FAITH

One of our neighbors in the DP`s Camp Foehrenwald were the family Da Silva, Portuguese Jews that lived in Tunis and Spain before living in Libya and Belgium during the WW2. Just before the end of the war, they were denounced by a neighbor, caught by the Nazis and sent to Dachau. A few days later the Americans took over.

The Nazis didn´t have time enough to eliminate them. Six months later they asked the Camp`s administrators if there was a mainly Jewish Camp and that´s how they ended up living in Foehrenwald and a few years later our neighbors.

Mr. da Silva also bought a Bolivian visa and was going to take the same vessel in Genova. They could not get a Brazilian visa so he planned to go to Bolivia first, establish some contacts near a formal border and, if not possible to enter legally with his family, smuggle all into Brazil.

One night at the Vessel Antoniotto Usodimare in the wide ocean he, Joseph da Silva, invited us for a glass of Port wine and we accepted.

On the first opportunity my wife asked them if they really were from Spain. At the Camp Foehrenwald we had heard so and because she never met Spanish Jews.

Joseph answered that yes they were from Spain but their ancestors had left Spain in 1828 and then wandered in Tunis, Morocco, Italy and Libya.

Their children were born in Libya; two boys. Then a short stay in Belgium.

Their story was very similar to other Jews except that they were Sephardim, did live in countries outside Europe and at home spoke a different language called ladino. He learnt Yiddish while at the Camp.

Joseph started telling, in broken Yiddish, his family story from Spain, starting in the 1820s.

First, he sort of embarrassed his audience. He gave his public a choice. What language do they want to listen: Yiddish, Arabic, Ladino, Portuguese or Spanish.

We selected to stay with Yiddish. Then he started telling a summary of his family`s history which was the same as millions of Jews, before, during and after the war.

One of his ancestors called Joseph da Silva, an astronomer and scientist as a main activity and writer and poet as a hobby was, in 1826, imprisoned by the Spanish Inquisition from the city of Valencia and accused of blasphemy, insulting God, denying that Jesus was the son of God and a list of other crimes.

The inquisitors prepared an elaborate ceremony. The complete parade!

Organized a procession, a specific mass at the city´s cathedral where all the local authorities and their wives enjoyed the evening, was requested and oath of obedience to the Church and to the holy inquisition by the religious authority, a sermon was shouted angrily by the local bishop and a sector of the bible read.

His ancestor`s agony happened to be the last Auto-da-Fe in Spain. He was eliminated and his family, wife and two children moved on to Tunis after losing all their belongings except the clothes they were wearing.

The inquisition had its first known victim in Paris in 1242 and its last in Mexico, 1850.For all time, six hundred years, the churches inquisitors persecuted Jews mainly in Spain and Portugal and then from their colonial states.

The most enthusiastic nationals with the Auto-Da-Fe were the Portuguese and Spanish.

Their victims were gypsies, crypto-protestant, Protestants, Jews and any other considered different.

One of the earlier Acts of Faith against Jews was in Paris in 1391 mainly targeting converted Jews, those called Marranos in Portugal and Spain.

Another important Act-of-Faith resulted from an uprising in Toledo in 1449.

I asked Joseph, and he was a well informed person, what he believed to be the reasons for antisemitism.

He thought for a while and answered:

"I think there could be three reasons:

The first one is the Crusades.

The second is the Law of the Purity of Blood.

The third is the myth of the Ownership of God`s truth; that is the scriptures or the written truth.

Let`s elaborate this theory: The crusades carried along tens of thousands of people of various origins, various nationalities for various reasons with one target: Free Jerusalem from Muslim hands. Those who went to Jerusalem for religious reasons, those who mixed religion and power, and those who expected to get rich and become landowners and obtain nobility titles.

This crowd had their leaders; military type, apparently ascetic, obsessive, from noble origin, but not normally heirs. Main inheritance and nobility title were left to the firstborn. The other brothers and sisters lived and ate at their parents homes; and received similar education but the first born male inherited most wealth and power.

Also went together agitators that in their madness preached hatred. Hatred for what? Hate for the difference. There was a big effort of uniting the Catholic Church around one pope on one side but at the same time hidden internal forces worked against this idea.

With regards to the Jewish people, in the city of Safed, religious leaders were already thinking that they needed the coming of the Messiah to take all Jews to Israel. Speculating about the Messiah coming and maybe not acceptable to the Jews, maybe to a few? Then these few would take the news to the people of Israel and maybe be successful. Most Jews worldwide would then return to Israel. The crusaders would find them happy but poor, loot their properties, rape their women and kill a few. And be satisfied for it since it was god`s will.

The Jews had been selected as the chosen people in the scriptures, what is the countermeasure?

Maybe they thought: As we have the power let`s convert them to Catholicism or if they disagree, eliminate them or expel from the country and keep all riches left behind. Weak point: converted Jews were sincere or just for survival convenience?

Being catholic for the public consumption and remaining Jews at heart? If not sincere then again the solution found was to eliminate them or expel. Not sincere is equivalent to treason and punishment for it is death but always with some suffering beforehand.

The second Theory was really racist: Purity of blood. Old myth, that differentiates via blood (genetic connection; family tree origin). To have purity of blood is a step to perfection and therefore God`s preference. From this you are better than others (if pure) if you descend from known Catholics who also descend from other known Catholics. Being better than others runs a risk of dirtying the pure blood.

One countermeasure to keep blood purity is to eliminate those different, forbid intermarriage or doubtful origins.

This theory may partly explain the racial question of segregating those different. If given a deep thought you come to weird conclusions. As an example: Jews were in Spain for about seven hundred years. As long as the Arab's presence from year 700s till nearly 1500s, and in general it was considered a golden period for Southern Spain.

Mixed marriages happened often enough to have thousands of children born with "mixed blood" and after so many years thousands of Spaniards had "Jewish Blood", same occurred in Portugal.

By the same considerations "Arab blood" must be widespread in the Iberian population.

If social scientists theorize that thirty percent of Spaniards have Jewish genes imagine how many have Arab genes. Practically the majority would.

So common was to have "Jewish ancestry" in Portugal that in Spain one nickname for "Jew" was to be called a "Portuguese".

This "Law" was implemented in a bloody manner by the Jesuits who started their existence being very hard line and thru the years became softer. This "Law" criterion of number of generations and others was also applied by the Nazis.

The third theory is who owns the truth. But not just the truth. We are talking of God`s given truth; for example the old testament, the ten commandments received by Moses. Some say that the Scriptures have God`s truth and this was given to the Jews or written by Jews under divine inspiration.

Remember that Jews have an alliance with God and the confirmation of this, same as a wedding ring symbol, is the male boy's circumcision. In the 1500's many popes tried to eliminate important Jewish religious books; Talmud and others.

Countermeasure, you forbid certain books, publish your own version and comments, eliminate or burn the other side's books. That is you try to vanish historical proofs so you can place another truth, new or modified. You eliminate from history your source of hatred.'

In the dark middle ages the church wanted to convince people that Catholic religious concepts were the truth and not Jewish. For these reason they promoted debates across Europe between Jewish and Catholic intellectuals where usually representing the catholic side was a converted learned Jew.

Usually a well-known Rabbi as an example. Their intention, the Catholic Church, was to minimize the importance of the Jewish bible and maximize the Christian bible and the presence of Jesus'

Joseph rested a few seconds and finalized:

-'In summary, antisemitism is a form of hatred, a way to channel your dark feelings that remain from pre-historical times in an inner part of your brain and the mechanics of this state of spirit is to select a target or targets: Jews, black people, Gypsies, Homosexuals and others; then direct all your energies to eliminate this source of dark feelings.'

Stopped for a drink and continued:

-'These dark feelings probably come from the times where humanity was still cannibal and at a certain stage of development, reason entered the brain cells thru a combination of chemicals and memories, and step by step eating each other was considered antisocial.

Maybe when men stopped living like a pack of hungry wolves and obtained food in an organized way. Like agriculture.

As long as we humans consider being different; be it skin color, behavior, education, beliefs, language an important trait then difference will prevail as a question of comparison. To be different then implies in being better or worse or superior and inferior than others?

To be different is just a strategy of nature because diversity gives more chances to survival as a result of the process of adapting to the variable environments and living conditions. That is all for being different'.

-'Would you and your family go back to Portugal or Spain?'- asked somebody.

-'No, I would not. What happened in WW2 lefts scars result of wounds that partially healed but remained as memory scars. Not only for what we personally lived but also for what we have learned from others and should not forget. It is not a matter of revenge, it is a question of never having again something like the Holocaust occur to any person or group of persons.

Time may heal such wounds and maybe my grandchildren or their children will return to Portugal due to interesting momentary conditions but I hope they know what happened and they work for it not to happen again'.

Anti-Judaism seems to be a more appropriate word than "Anti-Judaism'.

There was 'a specialized' collective hatred against Jews in Europe due to school teachings and church´s lectures that started in the early centuries after Jesus. In the beginning the clash between the established Judaism in the Holy Land then followed by friction due to the break up from main Judaism by Jews following another Jew who said he was de Messiah.

These Jesus followers, originally all Jewish started proselytizing and allowing into their new faith non Jews and received as answer prohibition to assist service in the synagogues, restrictions for marriage and other segregation actions. Thus created a new friction movement. Now conditions for religious revenge were ripe except where was the power?

Emperor Constantine solved this equation by becoming a Christian himself and making it the empire´s religion.

Once in power they worked to eliminate their foes and having at their disposal the help of also Christian chevaliers. For a Millenium things developed slowly until the top of the Church promoted the crusades;

Where crusaders become the armed wing of the cross representing some sort of Jesus armies with the purpose of recovering the Holy Land and divide it within European nobility.

The crusaders became religious faith fighters and discovered that they had effective power and resources.

Clean up for ethnic reasons started and political movements for country's unity became a goal for every king.

For the Pope, unity in Christ that permitted a territory to unify, was a blessing because the representative of Christ on earth was the Pope.

Modern countries were born and the process of reinforcing unity persisted as countries consolidated by acquisition and by force; and modern empires were formed (Austro Hungary, Russia, Ottoman, French and British,etc).

This left religion relegated to a secondary position in the power game so it searched for the 'common enemy'. The Jews were easy to find and became their common enemy. In simple thoughts explained my mental structure to try and understand anti-Semitic attitudes.

Before ending the evening one of the head of a family travelling to Bolivia asked to say something.

-'I am David and survived an extermination camp, Treblinka.

I wanted to make a correction on what was said a few moments ago and it refers to the idea of Jews being the chosen people. I was taught that our sacred books explain that God was selecting his chosen people and no group was accepting his offer because there were too many things and actions to be followed, behavior formulas, eating and even sex positions and attitudes.

It was said that nobody was accepted in the first round and the Jews were selected in the second round.

Then they were given the chore of practicing always 'Tikun Olam" roughly meaning to fix, correct, maintain, improve, the world.

Tomorrow we take the vessel to the port of Arica in Chile.

What would Giuseppe ask from us when we get established in Bolivia?

What should be our Tikun Olan? – finished David under applauses.

Please work hard and make a comfortable life so you can help others.

That will seek protection in the future.

Play hard so those able and willing can enjoy life fully.

Do not forget you are Jewish

These were the closing words for that day.

14-BON VOYAGE

"Antoniotto Usodimare" was the third name of the vessel. Originally constructed in 1942 and baptized under the name Sebastiano Caboto by the Cantieri Navale Ansaldo for Cargo Duties, was renamed in 1945 as Mauro Vicentini. In 1947 it was refitted for Passenger duty and renamed Paolo Toscanelli and finally launched in 1949 with the name Antoniotto Usodimare. With regards to passengers, it was qualified for one hundred and sixty eight persons in first class and four hundred and forty six passengers in tourist class.

The name Antoniotto Usodimare came from a well-known Genovese merchant who worked for the Portuguese Prince Henry the Navigator and discovered part of the West Coast of Africa in the years 1455-1456.

Its route comprised Lisbon as a start; after touching other ports in Europe, including Genova, went to the Caribbean and then, after crossing the Panama Channel, touched various South American ports in the Pacific Ocean, such as Guayaquil and Arica, until Valparaiso and then back.

We boarded in Genova, Italy. All four hundred and forty six tourist places were sold out and all were migrants with destination in the Caribbean countries, Panama, Bolivia and Chile.

Of these twenty families, all Jewish, had as port destination Arica, port city in the extreme north of Chile interconnected by rail to La Paz, Bolivia.

This rail system was built by Chile as a compensation clause from the peace agreement of the so called, Pacific war. A war that gave Chile about one thousand kilometers of land and coast leaving the war losers, Peru and Bolivia, first without a large chunk of land with mineral riches and the second without a coast.

These twenty families meant fifty five lives of which we were four lives (Mother, Father, Grandmother and me, already two years old).

The schedule was to stay at the hotel "El Dieciocho" three days under an "in transit' visa permit and then take the train Arica-La Paz.

Everybody had an entry visa into Bolivia obtained from people working for the Bolivian Consulate in Munich.

Five families had Tarnogrod as origin for their grandparents and only two were known to each other from before the War. The long voyage took care that they got to know each other well.

The voyage from Genova to Arica was without major events except excessive ship balancing by the vessel that caused generally spread sea sickness, repeated visits to the bathroom and overboard vomiting.

Although the vomiting, when the vessel was rocking, was in all corners of the ship, especially on those long corridors.

My parents told me that as a child while navigating the Atlantic Ocean I liked to drink Coca-Cola and throw the small, originally designed bottles, into the sea with my father's incentives.

-'Throw it far! As far as you can son!'

At the same time my mother complaining that I should not do it, do not go near the edge and that too much Coca Cola would give me stomach aches.

There seemed to inexist an agreement on this matter and discussions about this habit remained thru the complete trip.

Dressed in shorts with short boots and white socks, white long sleeve shirt and a dark brown jacket and already two years I spent my time running around with my parents running after me, throwing whatever I found overboard into the ocean.

My close friends, Norma and Adolfo, whose parents were our neighbors at the Foehrenwald Camp were not going to Bolivia; they remained at the Camp for another few months. Finally they managed to obtain entry visas to Chile. It took us various months to find out where they were and how to contact them.

So our trip was rather boring, because of lack of friends my age and, because one of my parents was on guard with me 24 hours a day.

I visited the Captain's deck, the machine room, the kitchen, the restaurant for tourist class, the life saving boats, the mini church, the front of the ship and the back of the ship. This was my favorite spot, the back of the ship because I could see the sea water being expelled by the propeller and things I threw disappear in the ocean.

Every time I drank a bottle of Coca Cola or any other soft drink I run as soon as I finished drinking, to the back section of the vessel and threw the empty bottle into the deep waters of the ocean.

My other activity was to play ball with the crew of janitors.

They had a lot of fun kicking the ball to me and cheered me when kicked it back. They always asked my father if I was a boy or a girl. Of course they knew that I was a boy but they preferred to tease me as much as possible.

The reason was that my mother wanted me to keep my hair untouched until two years old. A custom practiced by traditional Jews.

This custom has not a well-known origin. One of the best known is that Rabbi Isaac Luria a famous mystic from the 16th century in Safed, Israel; practiced this hair cutting ritual. (or non- cutting ritual!)

Others say that in the bible says (or somebody thought it said) you should not take fruits from an under a three year old tree so they explain this custom by association.

Safed is a mystical city that started to become a mystical center after the inquisition started its dark activities in Spain and the outflow of Jewish started.

Various Jewish sages moved from Spain and started to teach and practice Jewish mystical traditions.

Changing subjects somebody was writing some daily notes of events on the ship. This happened while on board the Antoniotto Usodimare:

After a small birthday party with some tiny cake, we went to the ship's barber and asked to cut my hair like a little boy. I cried non- stop for half hour while my father oversaw the barber's work. It did not hurt.

Just screaming and crying, out of general frustration. My mother had told me the story of Samson, the children's version, and when the bad people cut his hair he lost his strength. So this was going to happen to me soon. The crying was my way of expressing my unhappiness for not having been consulted if I agreed, or not, with the haircut.

Why "the children's version? Because in the adults version Delilah cheats on Samson by cutting his hair, but after he fell asleep after having had sex.

Delilah was really a night lady who accepted being paid for having sex with Samson.

Why children cannot decide these things by themselves? It was, in a sense, a way of control and in summary, intellectual slavery.

A child my age knows what is best for him! My mother is wrong when she screams at me and my grandmother is twice as wrong because she complains in Yiddish, which I understand, and some people look funny at us and others just smile and say something in Yiddish too.

After a few days there was a routine schedule for me: Got up and immediately washed my face and brushed my teeth. My mother would wash my body with a wet towel. Put clothes on. I selected which shorts and shirt and my mother normally approved. My Grandma always disapproved. Then I got dressed and my mother would always comment to my grandma:

-'How good looking her little boy is'- and went to have breakfast with my father. If I ate everything, then I had the divine right to receive, as a medal, a small Coke, drink it and throw the bottle overboard.

Then smile satisfied with my superpowers.

Back to the haircut.

Most of my hair was picked up by my mother and wrapped in a piece of paper and placed inside a brown colored envelope.

Later, when I stopped crying, sobbing and complaining, I found out that my superpowers were intact and that I looked funny when looking myself into the mirror at the men's toilet. Somebody with a photographic camera took photos as a business activity onboard. It is difficult to understand for adults the reasons behind crying during a haircut. I'll try to explain:

First, it was not my choice, nobody asked me; second, there was a chance of losing part of my superpowers, I was not sure but it was a good reason for crying and third I had to listen to the stupid talk of the barber.

Imagine if it is not unfair!

He imagined that because of my age I would behave like a trained dog or a baby that cannot speak. He spoke a language I could not understand. My father later explained that he spoke Italian.

I accepted, resigned, my situation after a short time because I imagined myself throwing thousands of Coca Cola empty bottles into the deep ocean. There was a non-written message in each bottle. The messages were thought individually for each bottle and mainly had to do with my freedom. When I grow up and become an adult I promised to write. First I need to learn how to read and write in Spanish. This is the language spoken in La Paz which is our destination.

Grandma insists I should learn Yiddish before Spanish.

This was the main reason and we could add the frustration of only having the solution of crying and not being able to use my superpowers and punch the barber in the nose and throw the scissors far away into the ocean. Revenge will be sweet!

Back to my superpowers and routines:

After the Coke bottle event, my father took me to the children's room where a few monitors took care of the small ones until lunch, three days a week, drawing figures, painting, having a cup of hot chocolate, only half cup, otherwise the children with superpowers would get too strong and takeover the vessel and throw thousands of bottles overboard, put their grandmothers in the kitchen to cook and wash the dishes. To avoid this, they serve only half a cup of chocolate.

Lunch time was the entire family together with other families because the tables were community oriented and sat at the same time over fifty persons. Lunch time was always a fight. I did not like soup but the Italians did. So we all must take soup.

-'Not from the dish'- said my mother-'use your spoon!'

They did not understand that children with superpowers did not eat soup. Never! To use the spoon was humiliating. I preferred not to eat!

My father intervened: -'No soup. No ice cream'. I ate nearly all the soup!

Adults did not understand this business of soup. To eat soup means you are weak and soft. So it is against superpower philosophy, especially children`s superpower to have soup in your meals.

For me there was one acceptable exemption. The corn soup. It was yellow and sweetish. Both these qualifications were in my preference list. Still this is no excuse for allowing adults to push their soups. Somebody said this soup was an American soup. Better. They helped my father win the war. I did not see the war but heard in my father's stories and he told me he fought in the war. He, his brothers, other persons called Russians and the Americans. The Americans were very important and always had chocolate bars. Maybe they also had superpowers.

It is difficult to be a child and keep hiding your superpowers. They blackmail you, need to eat what you dislike and have to go to sleep when the adults decide. I may accept this order to go to sleep after lunch but not coming from grandma. She is not my mother. She is my father's mother so she can tell him what to eat or dress or when to sleep. Not me; I have my own mother!

She is my grandma so she cannot give me orders. Not really, actually she gave orders when she wished and in the manner she liked; with the choice of Yiddish or Polish.

Still, next time I will attack her with my water power and wet her hair. She always wore a silk cloth on her head. If she ordered me again I will take it when she sleeps and hide it!

Every day I learnt more and more about my superpowers. I could not fly because my flying cape was not prepared for it. It was too short! I had the strength, that is why I ate chicken every day, but it was not enough.

I was learning how to swim; but suspended for the time being. Too cold said my mother. I could run faster than a mosquito. I could jump. I could piss far away too. But I needed to go slow due to the zipper that existed in most of my short trousers.

On the vessel I was a prisoner of grandma, who gave orders to my father. But the real big boss was my mother who approved, or not, everything. From what to wear to whom to play with.

I was eating everything every day and night. As my father said, I could feel my superpowers growing because of my behavior. Whenever we get to the city of Arica I will test my superpowers with grandma.

My father explained to me that we get off the vessel at Arica because it is a port city where vessels arrive and dock. On the other hand La Paz is located inland without any contact with the Atlantic or Pacific Oceans. No seaport in La Paz. No river transport in mass scale.

Then after a few days in Arica, we will take the train to La Paz where we are going to live.

There I will meet other children living in the same building where we are going to live. I was curious about living in a building. I never did before. My mother explained to me that a building is like many houses one on top the other.

It must be funny. Everything I do in the toilet falls down on our neighbors downstairs. This is really funny. On the other hand everything our neighbors, from upstairs, do in the toilet will fall down on us. Need to think about this.

Something associated to this that also worries me is if these things would fly instead of fall. What would happen?

At night, after dinner my father would read to me from an Italian children's comic magazine called "Pepito" that we found on top of a table in a restaurant upstairs.

Basically "Pepito" was a pirate-child with a roundish face wearing a large red hat showing a skull and two crossed bones at the front. He had long black hair.

He had always the same target: to fight against the evil Governor of the Island, Mr. Hernandez de la Banana also called "The Mortadella with legs" who had an assistant, the diabolical Scartoff. Pepito owned a ship named the Peanut and also had an assistant, named Crochette.

Also has a funny group of buccaneers and his parrot Bec-de-fer and a monkey called Parakeet and sometimes by his second name, Pancrace.

My father had been told, by some ship brothers he made on this trip, that they found an Italian version of a magazine for children that they saw in Germany in the DPs Camp being used by some children. Maybe your son could enjoy it they commented.

"Pepito" was published as part of the comics magazines "Gaie Fantasie and Cuccciolo" as a comics strip and I liked it very much because he was always the winner and the monkey Parakeet always did some monkey business and always defeated the Governor Hernandez de la Banana.

Every night, although we had only one copy of the magazine, my father would read a new story that he made up according to how tired I was or related to some conversation we had before dinner.

My mother enjoyed watching us while my father was reading this magazine and telling me a "Pepito" based story. She knew he did not read Italian; that nightly stories were invented but she enjoyed that the stories had a ship and a Parrot named Bec.

One day I asked my Grandma to play with me. She initially refused saying she was too old and sick. After a few minutes of insistence she agreed.

-'Grandma, you close your eyes and count until ten. Then you can start looking after me. I will hide and you try to find me'.

Grandma stood facing the wall and started counting in Polish until ten. Then she turned around and saw nobody near.

The game was called "hide and seek".

I explained it twice to Grandma.

She said she understood. She started looking behind the door, under the staircase, all around the promenade deck. She looked in every corner, opened every door until she was certain I was not there. Then she moved into the playing area and nobody there.

Started to get worried and looked under the lifeboats without success.

She panicked and quickly returned to my parent's cabin in the tourist section and then I thought I was lost. After disappearing and not being found my mother started screaming:

-'Where are you my baby?'- rapidly she and my father went up to the promenade deck and started calling and searching for me.

-'Where are you son? Come out of hiding please! Where are you son?' – My father kept on repeating.

I was listening to all this noise but let it happen for a few extra minutes. When everybody was very worried and upset and two officers from the ship were helping in the search I appeared from inside the lifeboat where I was hiding and said:

-'Hello!'

Slowly people started to appear.

First were the two officers that picked me up from the lifeboat; then some strangers followed by my progenitors.

They were very glad to see me but my father placed me under punishment for frightening my Grandma. The real situation was that I was placed under arrest in the cabin.

She was very upset and nervous sitting in the cabin when we arrived and she gave me a big hug. I saw her face and she had been crying.

-'Don´t worry Grandma. I am OK.'

-'Where were you hiding?' – Grandma asked.

-'Inside the Lifeboats'. But I promise not to hide from you again.' – I answered.

Next day I asked my Grandma if she wanted to play hide and seek. She agreed but under the condition that she hides first.

So I started to count:

-'1,2,3,4,5. Eleven, twelve and twenty'. Turned around and saw grandma open a door and enter. She left a small opening and the door unlocked.

-'Grandma, Grandma!' – I started to call while walking to this unlocked door, the room was a storage room for cleaning material for the deck.

I very quickly got to the door`s handle, pushed it until being closed and locked it. Sometime afterwards, I found the monitor´s room and started my activities there.

I was painting when my mother very upset arrived, asking me:

-'Have you seen Grandma? Did she bring you here? Have you seen Grandma?

All the questions were asked simultaneously.

I answered –'I did not see her. She left me here and left'.

My mother´s face went red and she started asking the monitor for my Grandma but she did not speak Italian and in German it took some time to communicate what she wanted. The older monitor got the message and asked me to show how I got into the monitor´s room.

I took him back to our sleeping cabin and walked all the way to the monitor`s room. He asked: where did we stop. I showed him where we stopped to play hide and seek. He went directly to the locked door of the cleaning material and opened it. Grandma was praying.

The monitor called my mother to come near the door and indicated to her where Grandma was. My mother entered the small room full of broomsticks and buckets and took Grandma by the arm and helped her out of the room.

-'He locked me in there'- she said to my mother.

-'Is it true?-'My mother asked me knowing already it was true.

-'I locked the door but I did not know Grandma was in there'- I answered. Then showed how to get to the monitor`s room.

Later at lunch and with me having to listen to my father`s speech, after getting a full report from my mother over the morning events, my mother said to my father:

-'Grandma cannot take him by herself any place. She cannot follow his games and it becomes very dangerous to leave both together alone. From now on one of us must be together'.

-'OK'- Answered my father smiling and turned to me,

- 'Son, you must be careful what you do with Grandma. She is old and you need to take care of her, help her; right?'

I agreed. With my superpowers it should be easy.

The days passed with a monotonous rhythm. Every day throwing the Coca Cola bottles into the Ocean, my mother complaining that this or that was dangerous, my father thinking on how to organize an activity for La Paz, Grandma getting each day more senile and my mother worried about everything.

Finally we arrived; the vessel blew its horn twice, and soon after two auxiliary boats were guiding our vessel into dockside. In less than thirty minutes it was docked and fixed to the docksides.

The Immigration officers came up and checked everybody's documents and passed thru an instantaneous check up by two nurses and one doctor who inspected everyone's tongue, teeth and eyes. If approved one of the nurses would give a small book/certificate. Then we could disembark.

Finally on firm land, finally in Arica.

We said goodbye to some families we befriended during the trip and who were going to continue to Valparaiso, the main Chilean Port. Their final destination was Santiago and some small cities nearby.

In Arica we spent the three days walking around and getting used to firm land after twenty two days at sea.

In these few days my father visited some shops, talked to local established Jewish entrepreneurs and wrote down in his memory that Arica was an option in case plans for Bolivia did not go well.

He spoke Yiddish, Polish, German and managed Russian; that is why he visited only Jews.

He did not know a word of Spanish and his fortune was a few thousand US dollars and some sets of Silver artifacts which he pretended to sell in Bolivia.

He had been told that in South America these artifacts were well paid and that it was difficult to find. High middle class had a demand for Silverware and it was considered a safe way to maintain value of money.

Day two was dedicated to walking up and down 21 de Mayo Street where for about five blocks, on both sides of the street, only shops were installed.

Talking to an owner of a shop he heard that the future will be in imports because the local politicians were planning with the central government to install a duty free zone that could attract buyers from Peru (Tacna) and Bolivia (La Paz) for competitive goods and some investors who would import parts, assembly locally and sell finished products like cars.

This day we went for a walk near the ocean. There was a plaza with children's games and many children there. Except father who spent all day researching and visiting the businesses in the commercial sector.

What everybody was talking would take a few years to happen if it ever did happen. It was something not thought about before in Europe as his business activity: imports. His question was who will buy the imports?

In the afternoon we took a tour. We started at the corner of 18th of September Street and Colon Street, walked a few blocks and were at the Saint Marcus Cathedral, mainly in steel plates and steel structure.

This steel cathedral was inaugurated in 1876 and it substituted the old Main Church of Arica destroyed in an earthquake followed by a Tsunami in 1868. Engineering and design made by Mr. Gustave Eiffel.

Walking down the Cathedral`s steps we were at Plaza Colon and going parallel to the coast we passed the building of Customs and few minutes later the train station of Arica-La Paz. After re-viewing the station for about half an hour we walked freely thru Arturo Prat Street until 18th of September St., walking very slowly we stopped at the corner of Patricio Lynch street.

Next to the corner was a small coffee shop with six tiny tables where we sat for a rest and to have coffee and soft drinks. My father preferred tea and if possible some lemon. In private he enjoyed his black tea with grapes!

We called the attention of the waiter and the coffee shop manager.

Our clothes, dressed formally like Europeans, had in them the message: "foreigners"! The manager`s name was Jorge, and after the waiter took our order, he approached our table and asked in Spanish:

-'Good afternoon, my name is Jorge and I am the owner of this place. Nice to meet you'- and he extended his hand to greet each one of us.

-'Do not speak Spanish'- answered my father -'Polish, German and Yiddish' and a little English.'

I repeated: 'do not speak English'.

-'Do you live in Arica?' - asked Jorge in Yiddish with a German accent.

-'No, We came from Europe, Germany to be exact, and tomorrow will use the train to go to La Paz, our final destination. We hope to find a peaceful city with friendly people – answered my father in Yiddish.'

-'Sorry, to ask so many questions. I am Jewish, and you?' – asked the manager.

-'Yes, we are Jews and we came from a DP Camp in Germany near Munich' – said Majer.

-'Sorry to ask but why La Paz' – he asked with a doubtful looking face.

-'Very simple, Bolivia was the only country willing to give us an entrance visa. That is why five families from the same Camp are going to La Paz'.

-'What do you do for a living?' – The manager asked.

-'Commerce, Buy and Sell; Import silver objects. But do not know if it works in La Paz. Probably any work until we figure out what is better and gives us a future' – stopped to think and continued' – 'I believe in the silver objects. They are very fine objects with Slovakian handwork and high quality silver. Pure silver' – I answered.

-'Pure silver, Pure Gold! The people from Arica have a legend about a bell that was found here in the 1930s and thru scientific investigation found out that this bell had been ordered by a wealthy businessman in the colonial days.

The people that found the bell tried to sell it to foreign buyers but police surprised them and as it was considered to be a highly valued piece, supposedly of gold and silver, as ordered by the rich gentleman; it was sent directly to be kept at the central bank of Chile, together with the nation's gold reserves.

Years went by and about ten years ago a campaign started, to recover for the city of Arica, this precious bell.

The central government denied sending back the bell saying that it was considered to be too valuable, pure gold and silver, and therefore too dangerous to have a piece like this exposed to the public and subject to exercising a big attraction with robbery experts.

A commission of the highest level was formed composed of the bishop, the mayor; he oldest judge and others and after a big dispute they managed to arm twist central government bureaucrats and got back the bell to be shown at the Saint Marcus cathedral. There was joy in the city of Arica and the bell arrived from Santiago heavily guarded to be greeted with week-long celebrations.

After a few weeks a technical survey was conducted on the bell to determine its real value estimated in many millions of US dollars.

Result was disappointing; the bell was made of normal bronze with a small amount of silver, like any bell.

Beware with local smart hoods!'

The third day arrived and we were all that evening at the train station, ready to board the "Ferrocarril Arica-La Paz".

This train line was inaugurated in 1913 with four hundred and forty kilometers of extension, crossed the Andes mountain range and reached the highest point at four thousand and sixty five meters above sea level.

On its way to La Paz it stops at more than twenty stations. It was built under the responsibility of the Chilean government as a result of the Peace Treaty signed in 1904.

People come up the train selling sweets, woolen head covers, gloves, corn cakes and water; at every station.

And we boarded the train, Majer, Roza, Grandmother Szjandla and myself; we all stayed in the same wagon and slept most of the trip although people came up onboard at nearly every station and knocked on the cabin's door offering handicrafts, sweets and soft drinks.

Soon after a long sleep we arrived at the La Paz Station where some friends from the Camp Foehrenwald were waiting for us. They had already rented an apartment for us in the same building as they lived.

They lived at the fourth floor; we did at the fifth floor. Overlooking a small plaza, with a few wooden seats, a water fountain in the centre and a few trees.

It was rather quick to get from the train station to the apartment and we travelled in two taxis because of the luggage.

As soon as we arrived to the apartment we brought up the luggage with the help of the taxi drivers and distributed things in the various rooms. The apartment seemed large after the weeks spent on the vessel and using as reference the Camp Foerhenwald´s accommodations.

-'This was going to be home for the next four years'- I heard my father say already planning to move further up.

In the next few days, my mother distributed the luggage and accommodated each of us in the rooms, one room for my parents, one room for my grandmother and another for me.

She then prepared things for the kitchen while my father went with our neighbor to meet other members of the Jewish community living in La Paz and listened to their opinions and comments. Back home for dinner we all had an explanation:

Everybody mentioned good business and bad politics.

Good business meant that there were few commercial facilities and demand was large. Street competition, which meant people sitting on the walk-path underselling everything, against installed and equipped shops.

After a few weeks, my father found two other Jews interested in doing business together with a similar project.

Their idea was to manufacture leather shoes and handbags for ladies.

Near home they found a house which in front could became a shop and at the back the manufacturing offices. They bought wooden forms for shoes, employed four people to cut and sew the shoes and handbags.

The leather was also purchased but it was expensive and delivered off schedule.

So, barely speaking Spanish, the partners decided to purchase leathers directly from the hunters in the jungle. Majer and Seilig went into the Beni jungle and met hunters and closed deals for the next three months.

Selected various types of animal skins, negotiated costs and dates of delivery. Delivery would be at the hunter´s base and Majer and Selig would come to receive the skins once a month.

The El Beni trip was to get to Trinidad from La Paz.

About six hundred kilometers to be driven by car leaving La Paz and driving to Coroico, then Sapecho, Caranavi, going thru the Pilon Lojas Indigenous Territory Park, then San Borja, San Ignacio de Moxos and finally Trinidad.

This takes about twenty two hours driving but they made it in forty eight hours stopping to eat and sleep.

In Trinidad they checked their last purchase and sent via truck to La Paz the skins and furs.

To complete the new order, they travelled by boat and by foot to Villa Alba where they selected and/or ordered the finest skins normally from reptiles.

The monthly trip would last normally about six days. Business in the La Paz shop was going well.

The third partner, Haim, was doing well in the production and he trained enough people to produce twice as it was producing. Pricing was very convenient and the financial return for the partners looked reasonable.

Just a few months after arriving in Bolivia on April, 1952, we heard shooting coming from the streets and from the plaza in front of our building.

It was Sunday early morning and the shooting already lasted for five hours. Shouting names and orders, fire guns and window glasses being broken continued until dark.

We had various windows shot and broken glasses. We spent all Sunday laying on the floor and under the bed in our search for safety.

Later we heard on the radio that a revolution occurred and that Victor Paz Estenssoro was the new president.

On October of the same year the government nationalized mining concerns. In 1953 a Land Reform occurs and popular militias are created to defend the MNR party in power.

Going back to that Sunday in April, 1952 ; my mother while trembling next to me under the bed because of the shooting and being afraid of having the apartment invaded by militias, swore to God that in Bolivia she will not live.

Neither she nor her family!

She mumbled most of what she was promising to herself but what was totally clear was that rapidly we would look for other horizons somewhere else.

On top of the world, living at an altitude of over four thousand meters, the rarified air that made difficult breathing was sufficient to make life uncomfortable. It reduced physical performance. This added to popular uprisings, peasant revolutions with shootings and killings periodically, made her decide on not having any tolerance.

-'We have to go as soon as possible. In Bolivia, I will not live'- Roza kept repeating again and again – 'we just spent six years in WW2 and I do not want myself and my family to spend another day in a war area again'. It was quickly becoming a mantra which as repeated to family and friends at all time and any place.

Just too many memories of the bunker and the Germans.

-'This is not what I dreamt while awake in the Bunker' – Roza thought – ' for sure it is not.'

It was a place with warm weather, no armed revolutions, no shootings everyday for any reason and friendly people'. Ina few additional seconds she was adding to her dream:-'and normal breathing air'.

She would keep repeating that she did not tolerate headaches anymore. Apparently altitude caused her headaches.

In her knees she carried the pain of the bunker.

Roza took a rare opportunity where Majer was out downtown; and her son playing at the neighbors downstairs with his friend Juan, to have a nap after lunch.

She just laid on top of the bed and closed her eyes.

Suddenly she began to daydream; we were arriving by ship in Arica's port and most passengers were on the deck watching the Umberto Usodimare approach the docks when, surprising everybody, a fire bomb exploded about one hundred meters ahead an about fifty meters high,

The first officer took the microphone and announced:

-'Docking has been delayed. The captain has ordered to guide the ship to a waiting location. There we shall wait for new instructions. Please behave orderly and obey orders from the officers'.

-'Why are we not docking?' – asked Roza.

-'Yeah, why are we not docking?'- repeated the little boy.

-'It is gossip but they say that within the passengers there are a few officers from the Gestapo hiding and flying away from victor's justice in military controlled Europe.

The information arrived from intelligence sources in Italy as we were approaching Arica.

The Chilean authorities worried about lack of security decided to quarantine the ship and nobody comes up or goes down. The crew officers assembled to take some action and coordinated by radio with Italian and local intelligence' – informed Majer.

-'They need to be caught now'- commented Roza –' me and another five ladies can search in all upper class cabins and see if there are any weapons'.

They put their light rain jackets and all walked in the direction of the officers' quarters. The captain just finished a briefing meeting so he could speak to the ladies with updated information:

-'No information on who may be these Gestapo members, we will remain

where we are until duly authorized by local authorities, every passenger will be interrogated and his belongings searched; suspects will be jailed and there will be a daily meeting in this room'- said the Captain.

-'Back to the sea is where we are going'- said Grandma speaking to me.

It moved with the waves but we slept every night. Now these animals want to kidnap this vessel.

We must not accept we have to fight until the end"- completed Grandma.

15-BACK TO THE SEA

It was the beginning of 1954 and cloudy in La Paz.

My mother was pregnant and, with orders from her doctor to remain rested and relaxed, which she.

Later in the evening she talked with my father and expressed her feelings.

- 'We did not go to Israel because of the shooting and lack of safety although your brothers and many cousins went there. Why should we stay here where they try to solve political questions by shooting each other? Let´s go away from here' – said Roza.

-'Where do you want to go now?' - asked Majer.

-'To the seaside, to Arica in Chile'- answered Roza.

Grandma was sitting against the wall, half listening half sleeping. But she quickly caught the subject in the air and mumbled:

-'Let`s go back to Tarnogrod. Guedalia and I had a good time there.' – Grandma said.

Roza answered:

-'Grandma, Tarnogrod and Poland are full of communists and the boss is Stalin. He hates Jews'.

-'I heard he is a good man'- said Grandma ignoring the rest of the people -'He goes to the synagogue every morning and puts on his tefilim. Every day! I am sure he is a good person'.

Again Grandma passed out and heavily asleep started snoring loudly.

Roza insisted: 'Like I said, Arica', and repeated – 'Arica!'

-'Nice and warm; a nice ocean, friendly people. Not so many Jews. So nobody would hate us'- Roza finished joking.

-'They do not need any Jews to hate them. They hate everything that is different from them. They forgive you if you convert and become one of them. At least they promise to'- Majer said smiling.

Discussion on the same theme became a daily subject, and after my mother having made her decision, all the possible pressure was on my father to find the ways and means to go to Arica.

Meanwhile Roza was pregnant.

With three months a small belly appeared and they decided to tell me the news. I was nearly five years old and it was a happy event to know I would have a smaller brother or maybe sister.

I thought to ask my mother to go together when she visits her doctor and ask if it was going to be a boy or a girl. The reason for this was that every time I asked about it they would answer:

-'We don´t know we need to wait'.

My mother Roza explained one day that it was like and egg inside her belly and every day it grew a little. Totally is would take a long time, nine months, she said. Do not remember but it seems to be a long time.

I asked what does the baby do all this time inside the belly and the answer was it swims in a special liquid and it feeds itself from my mother's food. So I have to pay attention that my mother must eat twice, one for the baby and one for herself. Then I started to ask very important questions every day:

-'Mammy, if the baby eats then it must shit. How do you clean? Does the baby use diapers?'

-'The baby eats a different kind of food that Mammy's body prepares. Mammy eats food and her stomach separates some parts only for the baby and these parts are liquid. There is a connection between Mammy and the baby and it is called umbilical cord and works like a conduit taking special type food from the Mammy to the baby. The baby eats all and grows a little every day. That is why the baby inside the belly does not shit or piss' - Explained Roza patiently.

-'I don't understand everything you explained. But understand that the baby does not piss or shit'.

The weeks went by and Mammy's belly every day got bigger.

until one day she wet herself and my father and the neighbors upstairs took my mother to the La Paz Clinic where the doctor who had been in advance phoned, was already waiting. I stayed with the neighbor downstairs who promised to take me to the Clinic later to see the new born baby.

My brother or sister.

Such a long time and they do not know. Maybe my parents know and they want to surprise me. I believe they think I prefer a brother. I did not say but I really prefer a sister. Different kind of competition!

Why? Because if she is a girl she will have her own toys; she will not play with my cars, my truck, my firefighter truck, my planes and my football. She will have dolls and girl's toys. Also she will not have my friends but her own so we can each play with our own friends.

That is why I prefer a sister but my parents don't need to know so that they do not change the baby.

Every month my mother was bigger and bigger. I heard the neighbors say that babies come with one full size bread under their arm. This baby must be a big baby carrying a big bread swimming in a lot of water.

The lady downstairs took me to our apartment to change clothes. She picked an all blue overall, a shirt and boots and dressed me up. After combing my hair we left to the Clinic and in ten minutes we arrived.

The neighbor and I found my father having a tea at the bar of the Clinic and together we walked up a few flight of steps until the third floor where the delivery a surgery rooms were located.

Thru a glass corridor we saw the doctor coming and behind him a nurse pushing a stretcher on wheels looking like a silver cage and a few seconds behind my mother on a second stretcher on wheels.

The doctor came to the door and congratulated everybody and said that mother and baby, a baby girl, were well just needed a rest, and both were having a nap. Thru the bars of the bed on wheels we could see a part of the face of the baby, reddish and twisted. Probably trying to shit.

They installed both my Mammy and my sister in one room in the fifth floor, only obstetrics floor. After totally installed, my mother in the room and the baby sister in the nursery, they let us into the room where my mother was sleeping. We had a look of her face and she looked well.

So we walked to the Nursery and found my baby sister shitting again. This time we were sure because a few minutes later one of the nursery sisters was cleaning her. Then fed her and put her to sleep. Back at my mother's room, the doctor came in and explained the delivery to her, emphasizing that both mother and baby were well but tired so they would stay two or three days at the Clinic to recover totally.

I went to the Nursery many times until I saw her moving her arms in the air and screaming for food. They picked her up and took her to my mother's chest for breastfeeding. It took the baby a few seconds to find the nipple, and as soon as she did, she grabbed with her toothless mouth and started sucking. She sucked strongly for some time and then fell asleep in front of the ladies and my father, who were there offering chocolates and small sweets to the visitors.

One of our neighbors, the lady downstairs, asked my father about the baby's name and he said Hinde Rivque in memory of the deceased grandmother, mother of my mother.

-'Which name will she have in Spanish' - asked the neighbor upstairs?

My father answered, Hilda Rebeca. Later my father explained what those names meant; Hilda the hard working girl; and Rebeca, the one that unites, brings together.

He said there will be a Kiddush next Saturday morning at the "Circulo Israelita de Bolivia", a Jewish Social Center of La Paz, where the baby would be named properly according to Jewish tradition with herrings and vodka for breakfast. Everybody was invited after the Shabbat service was finished.

The "Circulo" functions like a Jewish club that has also synagogue and it is connected to the long history of the Jewish people in Bolivia. By the way and for the record this is the highest located synagogue on earth, about three thousand seven hundred meters over the sea level.

The first Jews in Bolivia were supposedly converted Jews, Marranos, that left Spain during the Inquisition years. The purpose of the agents of the Inquisition in Bolivia, according to historical documents, was to eliminate totally the Marranos.

Jews originally worked in the Silver Mines in Potosi and were significantly involved in the foundation of the city of Santa Cruz de la Sierra. Still there were few until the early 1900s where a wave of migration came from Russia, Turkey, and Argentina.

The few days passed and my mother and my baby sister Hilda were already installed at home.

The baby cried all night for a week and we all slept very little. After a while the baby stopped screaming at night and only cried when she was hungry.

After a few months I had already made friends with Hilda and she recognized me by making a lot of noise when she saw me and stretching out her arms so I could pick her up.

By then I had nearly finished my superpowers plan and needed her to learn how to speak to be able to share it with her.

I could fly more or less, water power to wet other people and animals, I knew how to swim faster than fish, not all of them but most of them.

I asked my father to look in the newspaper stand in downtown if the sold copies of "Pepito" the Italian cartoon magazine but the only one he found and thought to be appropriate was "Condorito" and he brought me one.

"Condorito", the character, was a small condor who loved woman and was always getting in trouble cause of them.

At night my father would read to me the adventures of "Condorito". By the way "Condorito" was a Chilean cartoon character

Sometimes I helped "Condorito" get out of some difficult situations thanks to my superpowers. Normally I was already in bed when my father came +to read to me or to tell a story. Then sometimes a situation arose where the hero could not solve whatever problem they had and decided to give up. Just went to sleep.

In the magazine the story showed they solved the problems but really they did not. So this hidden secret was for me and my superpowers to solve and we did either flying, pumping water or swimming. While sleeping I could transform and solve all type of problems. Just one important item to be careful about:

-'No soup!'

The moment I saw my baby sister's face in the Clinic I knew she could be trained in having superpowers so we could do special things together.

Now we have "Condorito" as another source of problems to be solved and we need to research for others; because "Condorito" seems to be too much interested in women and those problems, just me and my sister alone with our superpowers, cannot solve. Too complicated.

Who was "Condorito"? He was one of my comic book heroes but grew up and started making it difficult to be considered a hero like us. Imagine started liking women!

Two items are now important: my baby sister needs to learn to walk and talk before using any of the superpowers. Also needs to be trained in avoiding soup except corn soup.

Time passed rather quickly and everything was going according to plan. My baby sister was growing and with nearly one year of age she practically walked by herself.

She still needs to support herself against a wall, a sofa, a door to stand up; once up she can walk and normally not fall on her rear end. Her walk is not fully erect and some unbalance comes from the diapers. If wet or full they weigh a lot and difficult the walking movements.

During this period and since Germany, the spoken language at home was Yiddish with the exception, when already in La Paz, of the cleaning lady that spoke a mixture of Spanish and Aymara and most of the speaking was done thru the sign language, a new version of their own.

Things started to change and Spanish began to be used as the standard language at home; when a nanny was employed then my mother was liberated of spending time at home and could start working at the shop, my father increased a lot his knowledge of Spanish by having contact with the general public.

Apart from the nanny, who was nearly exclusive for my baby sister, a maid that cooked and washed the clothes was also a contributor to this mixture of Spanish and Aymara. In some cases a pinch of Quechua was thrown into this new homegrown Esperanto.

My grandma gave the peculiar note; she continued to refuse to learn any other language than Polish and Yiddish. So her instructions to the maid were ignored but every so often she had to comply with Grandma`s wishes otherwise she wouldn`t stop nagging and insisting.

Periodically Grandma would swear in Polish. I wasn`t sure if it was really swearing, but it certainly sounded to be like that.

It was the last days of 1954 when my father took a trip to Arica and said to my mother that he would arrange things so that shortly we could move to live there.

He stayed most of the time in Arica where he rented half of the house of a Chilean family. He contacted a businessman whom he met in Germany and was a distributor of goods.

This businessman was already a rich man after the war and migrated to Argentina where he got established and looked for opportunities to expand his business.

He established a partnership with my father to import goods to Arica, city that was going to become a duty free zone.

Soon at the beginning of 1955 he had himself organized in an import shop and a manufacturing facility for bed linen with this main partner and at the end of April of that year when my baby sister was having his first birthday we were booked in the Arica-La Paz train to go to Arica.

Arica became a Duty Free Zone in 1958.

16 -ARICA, SAND AND SEA

On April, 24th, 1955; after passing thru various revolutionary attempts and on the exact day of my sister's first birthday, we (except my father who had been for nearly six month already in Arica, Chile; organizing to have an activity and a home and be able to receive us in grand style) left La Paz on the train with final destination Arica. In a cabin were my mother, my baby sister, myself and Grandma.

There was room in the cabin for another two passengers. In a matter of seconds the two people appeared; they were two "cholitas", local indigenous women dressed in typical clothes.

Many layers of dresses and under dresses, dark hair, wearing a black small hat and carrying cloth large enough to serve as holder of goods purchased in Arica and smuggled into La Paz.

The train was full and there were various persons walking up and down the corridor, looking thru the glass windows to see if there is an empty seat in any cabin. Whoever from us who dared to standup my mother and grandma would immediately yell asking where I was going.

The two "Cholitas" were sleeping seated until the one seating next to grandma started to wet the floor. What a horrible smell and nobody dared wake her up. After an hour, and the cabin stinking, Roza decided to speak loudly and one of the "Cholitas" woke up, opened one eye and asked if we had already arrived. Roza very diplomatically pointed with her finger to the floor where the "Cholita's" feet and shoes were and a mini urine lake had formed.

The lady said "OK" and continued sleeping.

My mother later commented that the "Cholita" probably did not get up after been awaken and did not look the urine under her shoes, because she did not want to lose her place.

Normal behavior it was since her companion, the other "Cholita", saw the situation and did not alert her friend nor did she wake her up. The "cholita" who was sleeping moved her feet and put both shoes into her urine lake. Her colleague continued trying to sleep although aware of the fact that her friend's shoes were getting wet.

Probably it was business as usual.

A few hours later the whistle of the locomotive started blowing and waking up everybody in the train. Many people in a hurry were carrying their packs and suitcases up and down the train's corridor in preparation for arrival. The inspector was also walking in the corridor banging in each cabin's door and loudly yelling,

-'Arriving in a few minutes' – Screamed the conductor.

- 'Don't forget your belongings and God bless you all'- again the conductor.

When we arrived it took a few minutes to find my father in the crowd.

He was there with two porters uniformed that worked for the Train Company and were there to carry our luggage and packages. The heavy cargo was inside trunks which would be released the day after.

We entered my father´s car and the luggage was taken in a small motorcycle-truck that also worked for my dad´s business. In less than thirty minutes we were home.

There, waiting for us in San Marcos Street, was a partially rented home which meant three bedrooms, a kitchen room and a living/dining room and finally two toilets. The house belonged to the Romero family and was composed of Mr. and Mrs. Romero and three teenagers.

He was an executive of the Public Phone Company and welcomed the extra cash from the rent although sharing his house. But he knew it would not be for long.

Leaving the house to the right and crossing to the other side of the street, in the corner, there was an ice cream parlor called "El Pinguino" (The Penguin) and walking down half a block to the left, a Cinema. If you left the home to the left down San Marcos Street and walked a few blocks you could see the sea at the horizon and before that the Church of Saint Marcus, designed they said, by Mr. Gustave Eiffel himself.

Roza was nearly happy.

My first year of school was in a kinder-garden class of the Catholic school San Vicente. Only one year. Then, next year, Public School half day and Jewish School the other half. The Romero kids taught me to read and write Spanish at home before it was taught at school. My parents learnt Spanish with practice on a day-to-day basis with the public and as a means of survival, and were not able to teach me at home.

At the San Vicente School I was admitted temporarily, and thanks to Mr. Romero´s influence, for one year only and for the Kindergarten class; which meant that after one year I would be seven years and could be admitted to prep school.

The Kindergarten was five or six blocks away from the Romero`s house and every morning at 07:30a.m., somebody would walk me up to the school entrance and then at 12 a.m. pick me up.

The first event in the school was, all the classes together in the big Gym Assembly Hall would sing the National anthem and pray.

After the prayer every class walked into their classroom where the teacher would start explaining, writing or reading some subject. In our case, the Kindergarten kids we prayed again and sang a few songs.

Next were the intellectual activities: Paint some figures in a paint book with my name written on the cover, cut with scissors figures drawn on a sheet of cardboard and put them together with some twisted clips and glue some painted figures onto a sheet of white paper with our name written on it.

Just before the end of the first half we stopped the activity and went to deliver it to the teacher. Everything was delivered, the painting, the glued figures that were cut off a sheet of thin cardboard. The teacher would check that the name was on and make some comment:

-'Very Good Johnny'- said the teacher

-'Need to be clean, Arthur. This is a mess!' – said to another pupil

-'Better do it again at home and bring it tomorrow'—insisted the teacher

I always had a good comment. I had learnt to paint, cut and glue at home with the Romero kids.

In the evening I would show my production to my parents and they always asked: how was my day. I recited the prayer that I learnt and that we prayed at school every morning.

It mentioned persons I never met before: the Father, The Spirit and the Holy Ghost and also Jesus Christ.

Roza, my mother, disliked the idea that being a Jewish kid I had to sing and pray as a catholic. She would ask my father if we could not go to the School and speak to the headmaster about this. We were very transparent with Mr. Romero and we asked him about his opinion and what he would do in our case.

He suggested to be patient and that one year would pass quickly and that in the worst case singing and praying were not negative things.

-'Next year I would be at the Public School where no religion was taught.'

My parents decided to wait and discuss between them before any action. We should not risk having the boy expelled from the school for any reason because he needs to be with other kids and improves his Spanish and anyway Mr. Romero was right, it was only one year or really nine months, if holidays are discounted.

One day I came back from school and while having lunch, my mother came and sat with us at the table and asked:

-'How was your day?'

-'It was fine except that I was punished for not singing aloud one of the religious songs' – I answered.

-'What punishment?'- asked my mother getting a reddish face.

-'To repeat ten times the Lord´s prayer'- I answered.

-'Ten times? And what did you do?

-' I sang.''

-'Then?'-

-'The teacher, who was a priest and, he ordered me to sit at a corner in front facing the wall and wearing a paper cone on my head. Everybody laughed at me'.

-'And the teacher?'- asked my mother.

-'He also laughed'- I answered looking straight into my mother's eyes.

-'Are you hurt?'- Asked my mother-'I will talk to your father when he arrives and Mr. Romero later.'

In the evening my father arrived and my mother started telling him my story at school. He was very upset and decided to get advice from Mr. Romero before any further action.

He went to Mr. Romero side of the house and found his wife. She was a school teacher for teenagers and participated in social movements. My father asked her if Mr. Romero could spare a few minutes in something important, referring to school for me.

When he came we were already chatting about the school events with Mrs. Romero and she summarized them to him. He was a very intelligent man and immediately picked up what was really bothering us.

The segregation of the boy in front of his classmates. Everybody, including the teacher laughing at him for not singing loud.

-' What a stupid action! Priests can be very stupid'- Mr. Romero said and looking straight into my father's eyes continued:

-'I would like to go together with you to talk to the headmaster and to that teacher-priest. OK?'

Majer accepted and Roza was relieved. -'Maybe they will get angry at you and at the boy, shouldn`t we wait and thinka bit more?' – Roza tried to weigh the options – 'maybe we should talk to other Jewish families?'.

'-No, The sooner the better'- said my father and Mr. Romero agreed.

-'If no counter action by the headmaster then it is better to get the boy out of school and my sons and wife can teach him at home. Next year he can go to a normal Public School.'- said Mr. Romero.

My mother and father apologized for causing so much trouble and thanked the Romeros for being so nice people. They agreed to go to the school next morning.

Next morning Mr. Romero and my father walked early in the morning to school.

At arrival they asked for the headmaster and were told he would receive them after the daily ceremonies of singing the National Anthem and morning prayers.

They sat and waited. Not so long afterwards, arrived the Headmaster; he was a priest dressed in black and white, wearing a medium size beard.

Majer thought "he looked like the Chassidim" and felt relaxed.

Mr. Romero started to talk but the headmaster interrupted saying we should go talk in his office. Which we did; we walked about one block inside the school until we got to his office where he had a large table. We sat and were served tea and cookies.

Mr. Romero interrupted the general chat that my father was having with the Headmaster to say that he wanted on my behalf an explanation to an event that happened with Majer's son yesterday, whereby the boy was treated with enormous lack of respect and inappropriate psychological torture by making fun of him in front of his colleagues by leaving him in front of his class, seating facing the wall and with a paper hat.

In summary, by public embarrassment.

He was aware of the event. It was reported by his teacher as gross misbehavior by the child therefore causing exemplary punishment.

Majer asked if that sentence made sense for a six year old child whose crime was to sing in low voice a religious song. He did not refuse to sing he just did not do it loudly. Probably, because of being shy.

The headmaster's face became suddenly white and serious and he said they knew the child was Jewish and probably declined to sing the religious song because it was catholic. That the school was catholic, we knew before enrolling him for one year.

This was acceptable discipline for a catholic school.

Mr. Romero asked for license to speak and said that he was catholic, went to catholic school, had catholic friends and never ever heard of such stupid justification for a mind troubled behavior of a teacher priest that takes care of little children from Kindergarten ages.

Mr. Romero insisted that the boy was mentally tortured and psychologically abused and that we ought to insist that the teacher be suspended and given a different job.

After re-education he could come back to take care of small children.

The Headmaster insisted that the reason for the problem was the boy and his Jewish education that made him not respectful of catholic ways. –'This is a catholic country and its values need to be respected'- he finished.

-'Since that is your point of view as Headmaster I have no choice but to retire my boy from your school'- Majer said.

That was last time they saw that Headmaster.

Five years later I saw him one last time when at a schools civic parade I won a first prize for a poetry I wrote, and got this prize from the governor of the Province and the priest Headmaster was there in between the local authorities. For sure did not recognize or remembered me. He was there representing the Catholic religious authorities.

A year later my father had bought and reformed a house for ourselves. Just for ourselves with four bedrooms, dining room, living room, kitchen, daily dining, internal patio and a small garden.

Roza became very happy.

That night, the first one in our own home, I dreamt with the Desert and the Ocean. A large sea, blue sky and lots of yellowish sand burning your feet and making you run quickly into the water.

We had planned in Germany to migrate to Israel, sand and sea.

We were now in Arica, sand and sea.

My parents were happy in Arica.

Happy in the broadest sense.

17- NANNY RITA

A few days after we arrived in Arica my father had the idea of employing a Nanny to take care of my sister and keep an eye on grandma. My mother preferred business than home chores.

Many people that my father already knew recommended somebody. Finally a young girl was chosen. Her name was Rita, a brunette with dark skin, that my mother chose.

Rita started working a few days later because my mother wanted to work together in my father's business instead of staying at home. Also my father had plans and for them to occur he needed somebody of trust, rapidly at the shop. That somebody was my mother.

Quickly my mother learnt the business activities, became fluent in the Spanish language, was able to talk to the shop's employees and negotiate with the customers.

My parents walked around thirty minutes from home to get to the shop and spent the morning from 9 till 12:30 a.m. there, closed from 12:30a.m. Until 4p.m., went home had lunch, read the newspaper and had a "siesta" of about forty five minutes to one hour.

Sometimes, after he bought a car, Majer would buy some fresh seafood or fish for lunch or for dinner.

By then a new employee was added; Zuni was the name of the new employee who took over as a cook and was normally supervised by my grandma who was always physically present or at distance; Grandma tried to impose her opinions that nobody listened to, but always got a yes as an answer.

Nevertheless, not always there was a consensus with food.

When Zuni cooked tripe, spicy tripe with carrots and potatoes, my father walked away from the dining room and ate in the kitchen table together with Grandma. He just hated the smell of tripe but my mother loved it. In this case I followed my mother's taste.

On the other hand when Zuni prepared seafood, prawns, sea orchids and others, it was my mother's turn to share the kitchen's table. My mother's upbringing in her parents strict kosher home, made her dislike for life most non- kosher food.

Although she would eat non-kosher food in a restaurant, she never tried pork, prawns or other traditional seafood like lobster or octopus.

As already informed all home cooking activities were supervised by Grandma.

She sat on a stool against the wall next to the door and watched what was going on in the kitchen, while Zuni prepared the meals and where Rita prepared a snack or baby food for my sister. Sometimes my sister would get her food sitting on a high chair in the Kitchen because Rita wanted to chat with Zuni and my sister liked the movement of people there.

All these busy people, being watched, from the high chair by my little sister, Hinde.

In minutes, my sister's lunch was ready and it was placed on the high chair's front tray. Next, Nanny Rita put a plastic cup half filled with orange juice.

It was lunch time same as every day. Zuni had prepared the soup for my grandmother and she was eating at the same table in the kitchen, sitting on the supervisory stool. She finished her soup and got next dish of chicken breast cooked, same used for the soup, with mashed potatoes.

All this care for grandma had a reason: her teeth or lack of them.

Nanny Rita would sing and my sister ate a spoonful of mashed potatoes, cooked carrots and chicken meat. Every time that my sister refused the spoon, nanny Rita complained and my grandma complained too.

Except that, as it has been repeatedly said, Grandma did not speak Spanish, which was the current language used in the kitchen. She understood something but didn't care to make an effort to understand and spoke in Yiddish and Polish; especially the swear words in Polish were 'Oh Kurwa' and "Skurwysyn" directed repeatedly to Zuni, to Nanny Rita and to anyone that would not listen or obey her.

After cursing in Polish, she would mumble something, stand up from the stool and walked to the high chair where my sister sat and pinched her cheek. Immediately my sister started to scream and my Grandma returned to her stool smiling and sat there with her back touching the wall. It was her preferred practical joke. She really enjoyed doing it but nobody else.

This cursing, stand up and pinch activity, repeated itself three or four times per meal. In the middle of this event my parents would walk in and I would arrive from School.

My father walked into the kitchen, said hullo, left the keys from the shop on top of the table, said hullo with a kiss to his mother and went to wash his face and hands in the bathroom, My mother's entrance was similar. She walked into the kitchen, said hullo asked my Grandma in Yiddish how she passed the day, received the same answer every day saying in Yiddish that Zuni and nanny Rita were misbehaving, that both had boyfriends, that they brought them into the house while my parents were out.

Zuni would put the table at the daily eating room next to the kitchen and we sat for lunch.

After my sister Hinde had finished her meal and drank the orange juice, she would come down from the high chair, walk in the direction of my grandma and quickly pinched her near her knees and run away to seek protection from us.

Meanwhile my grandma complained in Polish 'Oh Kurwa' and other vulgar curses.

Which, my mother answered in Yiddish asking her to calm down. This went on daily. One day when Hinde was about four years and still Zuni worked at home and Nanny Rita took care of my sister. Lunch was finished and we were at the table eating fruits for dessert when Hinde came running into the dining room and frightened said that grandma is dying and Zuni asked for help.

Grandma was choking with something in her throat, she made some strange noises and she swallowed whatever she had stuck in her throat.

Her face was deep red and she was very upset.

What had happened? Grandma was sleeping seating in her stool in the kitchen when Hinde finished lunch, and saw Grandma sleep with her head backwards touching the wall and a full open mouth; Hinde picked my father´s keyring with two or three keys, and put them inside Grandma´s wide open mouth; she started swallowing, stayed in her throat and out of despair she woke up and swallowed the bunch of keys.

Grandma jumped off the stool and was running after Hinde who was hiding behind my father while Grandma wanted to grab her; my father picked her up and gave her to my mother who was choking with laughter.

My father got very upset and immediately called his doctor, Dr Granados, who asked to meet him at the hospital that was located at three or four blocks away.

My parents, Majer and Roza, took grandma to the hospital, ten minutes away; where the doctor managed to obtain a quick x-ray and verified that the keyring with the keys were there inside the stomach. He suggested the traditional stomach washing process and after some minutes the keys were delivered complete and properly washed.

My Grandma stayed a few hours for observation at the hospital and returned home to supervise, from her stool, the kitchen.

18 – THE CHOLITAS

Already gone one year, since we arrived In Arica from La Paz.

I was enrolled in the Public School, primary school, "Escuela Primaria Republica de los Estados Unidos de America" at a walking distance from home.

My sister Hinde was already two years old; she continued with her nanny, Rita. Grandma still dedicated to supervising the food and speaking in Yiddish to the cook, Zuni.

My mother worked together with my father at the shop. There were two other attendants, one senior and the other more like a messenger boy. The shop sold imported goods of all types: watches, jeans, women's wear, and many other popular items. Arica was a duty free zone.

Clients came from places were imports were restricted or at high import duties, mainly from La Paz, Tacna, Iquique and Santiago.

The shop was rectangle shaped, of about thirty meters deep and six meters wide with a balcony in L-shape leaving a rather large circulation area.

One day Mr. Santiago, the senior attendant of the shop, was selling some goods to two "Cholitas", dressed in their typical attire: black hat low topper type, printed blouse, shawl, various layers of colored skirts that nearly reach the floor. Not really an Inca fashion for indigenous Bolivian women.

But history tells that it was King Charles II of Spain in the XVIII century imposed this "Bolivian" look based on Spanish country girl's fashion.

It was the "Cholitas" job to be the building bloc of informal commerce in Bolivia. They sold everything; handicraft, food, flowers, fruit, clothes, dolls and everything else.

These two "Cholitas" carrying each on their back a baby, maybe two years old, entered the shop and greeted Santiago and my mother who was standing behind the counter got a bit closer to listen to their talk and see how Santiago manages.

Both wanted to buy women slippers, silk imitation men ties, baby pajamas and watches.

One at a time started negotiating the price of each item for four or five units. After some negotiation they reached a unit price, then, one of the "Cholitas" asked for a discount if instead of five units they bought eight.

After Santiago argued that the unit price was the same they wanted another additional discount which after some discussions and threats to give up, they nearly always obtained.

Then entered the negotiations the second "Cholita". She wanted another discount for twelve units instead of eight. She got interested but wanted an additional price reduction; they resold in La Paz so they needed a low price from the shop. Santiago said he was giving up. He swore that the price obtained was bottom price.

The "Cholitas" insisted and to make it convincing they would take a dozen units of another item.

Santiago complained that they were leaving the shop without a margin.

So if a nice discount on the third item they will take six units of a fourth item. And so it went on until they had bought everything they needed and my mother entered the circuit asking them from where they were.

-'From La Paz'- A Cholita answered.

-'How often do you come to Arica?' - Roza asked. -'About once a month'- answered one of the "Cholitas.

-'Since when are you doing this?' – asked again Roza.

-'Five years already'-answered the second Cholita.

-'How much do you spend here?' – Roza questioned.

-'About one and a half thousand American dollars each' – answered the "Cholita". -'You carry the baby at the back, how do you manage to carry all these merchandise? - continued Roza.

-'Some packages we carry together with the baby, the other packages we pick them up thru another person who comes into the shops and takes them to the railway cargo system; where he dispatches them and gives us the documentation to pick them up in La Paz.

Over there are our husbands waiting or at least somebody from the family to help take the goods home and next morning we are on the street selling to the general public' - explained the Cholita.

-'I lived in La Paz'- said my mother –'and when we came by train we were in a cabin with two ladies who looked just like you two'. -'We all look alike'- we are from La Paz. We need to go. Thank You'- said the other Cholita in a hurry. Immediately both paid and waved goodbye. The two "Cholitas" with their babies tied up at their backs and carrying some packages in their hands, left the shop after standing there for nearly two hours negotiating. Then Santiago said to look everywhere; where they were standing all the time, a small lagoon of liquid formed on the floor.

Santiago said smiling: -'Somebody pissed on the floor'. Then he and his assistant picked up two broomsticks and some old cloth and dried up the floor. Then they swapped the floor with water and powder soap twice to clean and get rid of the bad smell.

-'Well' – said Santiago – 'after all these years it has happened to us too. Many in Arica have been lucky to get this blessing from the "Cholitas". -'I do not want them here again' – said mother. -'Mrs. Roza, we need patience and tolerance, they understand things slightly different from us. Their mentality does not consider to urinate standing on somebody's house or office, a negative thing. Mind you she wore four or five skirts that got wet and probably her panties are also wet'. The baby they carry on the back makes all his necessities there and it does not complain. So what I am trying to say is that pissing like that is a cultural trait of the "Cholitas'" – ended Santiago.

My mother thought about her next words, inhaled deeply and started her speech: -'Santiago, never again allow anyone to piss inside the shop; If you see those two "Cholitas" tell them they have been banned to enter this shop".

-'Yes, Madam' – answered Santiago.

-'I will also talk to them in private to avoid being considered a tool of torture '- and turned around and looked to me: -'Do you piss on the floor or you know how to go to the toilet?'

-'I know how to peeh and pooh'- I answered.

-'Good on you fellow' – said Santiago smiling.

My mother`s last comment that day was:-'OK, we have been blessed by the "Cholitas" now it is lunch time. All are invited to go to the restaurant and have salteñas and a drink'- said mother after realizing how different her worries were now.

THE END

19-BIBLIOGRAPY

1-A Brief Short story of Poland-by Tim Lambert- World History Encyclopedia.

2-Wikipedia (checked many subjects); especially HEART (Holocaust Education & Archive Research Team) publication "ZEGOTA –The Council for Aid to Polish Jews – Guest Publication – Hans Stanislav Kopec -Gdansk.

3-America and the Survivors of the Holocaust-by Leonard Dinnerstein-Contemporary American History

4-Jewish Life in liberated Germany-by Koppel S. Pinson – A study of the Jewish DPs

5-Kibbutz Buchenwald- by Judith Tydor Baume – Survivors and Pioneersl

6-Rebuilding Jewish identities in Displaced Persons Camps in Germany - by Françoise Ouzan (On researchgate)

7-The Fascist Concentration Camps-From Internment to Deportation-Concentration Camps in Italy- by Carlo Spartaco Capogreco – University of Calabria

8- History of the Jews in Italy –From Wikipedia

9 - The Jewish Religion: A companion –Oxford University press

10 – United States Holocaust Memorial Museum – Foerhenwald

11 – Kidush Hashem – Cronicas Hebraicas sobre as Cruzadas – EDUSP- by Nachman Falbel.

12 – Guide to the records of teh Displaced Persons Camps or Centers in Germany 1945 - 1952

20 - GLOSSARY

1- Anti-Semitic: One who discriminates against or who is hostile or prejudiced against Jews. Adjective related to anti-Semitism.

2- Auto-da-Fe : (Portuguese) Act of Faith. Actions by the Holy Inquisition.

Public Ritual of Penance supported by Catholic Church.

3- Aliyah Bet : (Hebrew) Code name in Hebrew for illegal Immigration.

4- Aguaratumpa: God of destruction (Chiriguano beliefs)

5- Bamidbar : (Hebrew) "in the desert". Numbers biblical book.

6- Bund:(German) Secular Socialist Jewish Movement.

7- Brit Milah : (Hebrew) Jewish circumcision. (Also Bris in Yiddish)

8- Betar : (Hebrew) Right Wing Political Party / Movement.

9- Belzec :Extermination Camp in Poland. Start of implementation of Reinhard proyect to eradicate Polish Jews.

10- Bo Skurwysyn: (Polish):curse word meaning son of a bitch,whore.

11- Bolsheviks : Soviet Political Party under its leader V.I. Lenin

12- Beni Jungle : Jungle in Bolivia near border with Brazil.- Amazon region

13- Cheder (Yiddish):Elementary traditional religious Jewish School where basics of Judaism are taught.

14- CHOLITA (Spanish): Typical Bolivian indigenous women.

15- Chassidei Ashkenaz – Jewish movement,mystical, ascetic -12/13th century – in the German Rhineland.

16- Chiriguanos: Tribe of Tupi-Guarani origin

17- Esperanto: Artificial language created in 1887

18- Goyishe: (Yiddish):Gentile; Non-Jew.

19- Ghetto: City region where minorities are forced to live.

20- Haganah: (Hebrew) Israeli army.

21- Hashomer Hatzair: (Hebrew) Young Jewish Guard group.

22- Hospitaliers: Order of Knights of the Hospital of St. John in Jerusalem

23- Hassidism- Jewish movement that arose as spiritual revival in Ukraine in the 18 th century

24- Hassidim – Ultraorthodox Jewish religious group

25 – IRGUN (Hebrew) – Zionist paramilitary organization that operated in Palestine (1931-1948)

26 – Jagienollian: Dinasty founded by Jogaila, the Grand Duke of Lithuania who in 1386 was baptized as Wladislaw.

27 – JDC : Joint Distribution Committee –Jewish Humanitarian Organization

28 –Kaddish: Burial / mourning prayer

28a- Kiddush (Hebrew) :Sanctification over wine.

29 – Kippah: (Hebrew): Skullcap.

30 – Kibbutz/Kibbutzim (Hebrew) Collective farm.

31 – Kopecs :Polish currency,

32 – Kristallnacht (German) – "Night of the broken glass". Nazis in Germany torched synagogues, Jewish owned shops and homes.

33 – Mitzvot :(Hebrew): Commandments; good deeds.

34 – Maccabeans : (Hebrew)Leaders of Jewish rebel army (164 BCE).

35 - Mufti (Arabic): Islamic Scholar – Interpreter of religious law

36– Mikveh : (Hebrew) : Jewish Ceremonial religious bath.

37- Minyam (Yiddish)-group of ten Jewish adults required for religious obligations.

38 – Mortadella (Italian) : Cold meat cut. Normally used for sandwiches.

39 – Mohel (Hebrew) Circumcision religious specialist.

40 – Mizrahi - (Hebrew) Jews original from Middle East. (Oriental Jews)

41– Marshall Plan : American initiative to aid Western Europe after WW2

42 – MNR: Bolivian National Revolutionary Party

43 – Non Tolerandis Judaeis : Government decree for "Jews Free Zone"i.e.,Jews could not exercise functions, work or do business.

44- NKVD: Soviets People´s Commissariat. Russian Intelligence Service.

45– Oh Kurwa!: (Polish): curse word/expression meaning whore, prostitute.

46 – Pilsudzky, Josef – Polish statesman, revolutionary, Marshal (1867-1935)

47– Progrom: (Yiddish) – Violent attack with the intention of massacre or persecution of an ethnic minority.

48 – Partisan: Freedom Fighter against invaders of Poland.

49 – Peyes: (Yiddish): Sidelocks.

50 – Rosh Hashanah: New Year for Jews.

51 – Ruthenians: Ukrainians.

52 – SA : Armed branch of the Nazi Party

53 – SS: Armed Nazi organization

54 – Seleucid : Helenistic state that existed after Alexander the Great

55– Safed: one of four sacred cities of Israel. Kabbala center of studies since 16th century

56 – Samson – Ancient Israelite known for his strength (Book of judges)

57 – Sandek (Yiddish) Jewish godfather that holds the baby during circumcision.

58a – Shiva: 7 day Jewish dead mourning

59b – Shloshim: 30 days literally. Related to Jewish mourning too.

60 – Tefillin: (Hebrew) :Small square leather boxes containing scriptural passages worn in the front of the head and on the left arm.

61 - Tsunami (Japanese): Gigantic sea wave result of ocean earthquake.

62 – Tallit: (Hebrew): Prayer Shawl.

63 – Tzitzit: (Yiddish):Ritual fringes.

64 – Tumpaete : God of good (chiriguano beliefs)

65 – Talmud : Sacred Jewish book that registers subjects of Judaism

66 – Treblinka :Extermination Camp in Poland

67 – Tarnogrod :Small town in Poland

68 – UNRRA – United Nations Relief and Rehabilitation Administration

69 – Yiddishe Cheder: Jewish School.

70 – Yiddish : historical Language of Ashkenazi Jews – Central Europe (Originated in the 9th century)

71 – ZEGOTA: Polish Council to Aid Jews –An underground Organization created to save Polish Jewish people during WW2.

72 – Zionists: Nationalistic Political movement of Jews that supports re-establishment of a Jewish homeland

Others,

73 – Arica, Chile – Coastal city located in the extreme north, important Port infrastructure.

74 – La Paz, Bolivia – Most important city of Bolivia- located at nearly four thousand meters over sea level.

75 – Santiago, Chile – Capital city located two thousand kilometers south of Arica .

76 – Tacna, Peru – City in the extreme south of Peru near Arica.

77 – Bube – Grandmother (Yiddish)

Printed in the United States
By Bookmasters